BARBECUE
INFERNO

Also by Dave DeWitt and Nancy Gerlach

The Fiery Cuisines
Fiery Appetizers
The Whole Chile Pepper Book
Just North of the Border
The Habanero Cookbook
Heat Wave: The Best of Chile Pepper Magazine
The Pepper Pantry: Habaneros
The Food of Santa Fe

BARBECUE INFERNO

Cooking with Chile Peppers on the Grill

DAVE DEWITT
and
NANCY GERLACH

Ten Speed Press
Berkeley   Toronto

Complete copyright information for excerpts used continues on page 184.

Ten Speed Press
PO Box 7123
Berkeley, California 94707
www.tenspeed.com

Distributed in Australia by Simon and Schuster Australia, in Canada by Ten Speed Press
Canada, in New Zealand by Southern Publishers Group, in South Africa by Real Books, in
Southeast Asia by Berkeley Books, and in the United Kingdom and Europe by Airlift Book
Company.

Cover design by Paul Kepple
Text design and composition by BookMatters, based on a design by Nancy Austin
Food styling by Wesley Martin

Library of Congress Cataloging-in-Publication Data
DeWitt, Dave.
   Barbecue inferno: cooking with chile peppers on the grill / Dave DeWitt and Nancy
      Gerlach.
      p. cm.
   Includes bibliographical references and index.
   ISBN 1-58008-154-1 (pbk.)
   1. Barbecue cookery. 2. Cookery (Hot peppers) I. Gerlach, Nancy. II. Title.
   TX840.B3 D49 2001
   641.5'784—dc21   00-037793

First printing, 2001
Printed in Canada

1 2 3 4 5 6 7 8 9 10 — 05 04 03 02 01

Dave:
This book is dedicated to the memory of my father,
Dick DeWitt, a griller way ahead of his time.

Nancy:
I dedicate this book to Jeff Gerlach,
my partner at the grill and in life.

THE SCOVILLE SCALE

Scoville Units	Chile Varieties and Commercial Products
100,000–500,000	Habanero, Scotch bonnet, South American *chinenses*, African birdseye
50,000–100,000	Santaka, chiltepín, rocoto, Chinese *kwangsi*
30,000–50,000	Piquín, long cayenne, tabasco, Thai *prik kee nu*, Pakistan *dundicut*
15,000–30,000	De Árbol, crushed red chile; habanero hot sauce
5,000–15,000	Early jalapeño, ají amarillo, serrano, Tabasco sauce
2,500–5,000	Mild jalapeño, mirasol, large thick cayenne; Louisiana hot sauce
1,500–2,500	Sandia, cascabel, Yellow Wax Hot
1,000–1,500	Ancho, pasilla, Española, Old Bay Seasoning
500–1,000	NuMex Big Jim, NuMex 6-4, chili powder
100–500	R-Naky, Mexi-Bell, Cherry, canned green chiles, Hungarian hot paprika
10–100	Pickled peperoncini
0–10	Mild bells, pimiento, sweet banana, U.S. paprika

Acknowledgments

Thanks to the following smokers, grillers, and barbecuers for their help with this book:

Pat Chapman
Jeff Gerlach
Dennis Hayes
Sharon Hudgins
Kellye Hunter
Neil and Sandy Mann
Denice Skrepcinski
Melissa T. Stock
Carolyn Wells
Mary Jane Wilan

Contents

Recipe List

FIVE

For Carnivores Only

EIGHT

Spiced-Up Seafood
Infused with Flames and Smoke

NINE

The Meatless Grill
with Elevated Heat Levels of All Kinds

TEN

Super Spicy Sides and Some Grilled Desserts

With Revelations about the Authors and Our Definitions of Barbecue

AT AGE SEVEN, coauthor Dave got his first lesson in grilling. It was a Sunday afternoon in the early 1950s in Falls Church, Virginia, and Dick DeWitt, Dave's dad, was engaged in the newest suburban ritual: attempting to grill fatty chicken pieces over charcoal without burning them. Dick, who had acquired a family reputation for burning the chicken, suddenly handed the tongs to Dave and said, "I'm going to get a beer. Be right back. Watch the chicken." He walked into the house and the phone rang. It was his boss at the Pentagon. As the conversation dragged on, Dave made a valiant attempt to save the chicken. He noticed that the coals were hottest in the middle, so he placed the thickest pieces of chicken there. Then he realized that the chicken parts had to be turned often or they would burn. They also tended to burn when the fat dripped on the coals and produced flare-ups. So he moved the dripping pieces to the outer edge of the grill where the fire wasn't so hot. Sweating profusely, Dave wrestled with the chicken for fifteen minutes until his father returned.

"Hey, you didn't burn it," Dick DeWitt said. "What's your secret?"

"You gotta watch it every second," Dave replied, a big lesson learned.

Now, forty-eight years later, you can adjust your gas grill to precisely the right temperature so the chicken supposedly won't burn. And even though you might not have to watch it every second, one of the fun things about grilling is that you do have to pay attention. With smoking, constant attention isn't as crucial, and some people have been known to take naps during the process. Okay, maybe they passed out while demonstrating the close affinity between outdoor cooking and beer.

Nancy's story is just the reverse of Dave's. In her nonbarbecuing family, nothing more exotic than the usual burgers and steaks got grilled. When she and Jeff were newlyweds, living in an apartment in the Berkeley/Oakland area, they would haul a small hibachi up the fire escape to the roof so they could grill. When Nancy first started grilling, the clouds of smoke that could be seen across the bay in San Francisco were testimony to the fact that she didn't know what she was doing. Being from Wisconsin, Jeff grew up grilling bratwursts, so he stepped in to show her the ropes, an arrangement that has lasted to this day: Nancy creates the recipes, does the prep, and Jeff does the grilling and smoking. In other words, Nancy sits back and enjoys a cold one while he does the work!

This is the ninth book we've coauthored since 1984, and we're still having fun! This one is designed for people with a certain amount of knowledge about outdoor cooking. It is not intended to cover the basics, like how to start a charcoal fire. There are dozens of books that will teach you Grilling 101, or you can ask your father. Likewise, we're not going to tell you everything we know about chile peppers. Please see the Bibliography under our names for our books on chile gardening, identification, healing powers, use in world cuisines, and just about any other topic you can imagine.

Enough about what this book isn't. It *is* specifically designed to prove that outdoor cooking and chile peppers are inextricably linked. All you really need to use the recipes and techniques contained herein is a passion for chile peppers and a love for barbecue, in all its meanings.

We use the word "barbecue" in three ways. First, and in the most general sense, it is a gathering of people where food—especially the meat—is cooked outdoors rather than in or on a stove. At most family barbecues, the meat is grilled; that is, cooked on a grate directly over the heat source. The second definition of barbecue, in the technical culinary sense, is meat cooked indirectly from the heat source and flavored with smoke. Finally, the grilling unit itself, whether it is simple or full of bells and whistles, is called a barbecue. Oddly enough, the unit used for producing true barbecue is not called a barbecue but rather a smoker or a pit. Go figure.

—A Brief History—
The First 400 Years of American Barbecue

When the European invaders brought livestock to Mexico, pigs and sheep and cattle, the meat of these animals was cut up to be roasted over the barbecue frames, and the barbecue in the Caribbean became an outdoor feast equivalent to the clambake in New England. The custom would travel north, into colonial Georgia and Maryland and Pennsylvania, and the Spanish colonizers would take it as far west as California, where in time the spicy-hot sauces or moles of Mexican cooks served over roasted beef or pork would become eternally known as "barbecue sauces."

—Betty Wason, *Cooks, Gluttons, and Gourmets*

Now, a word about chile peppers. Both of us were grilling long before we discovered chiles, but as soon as we found them, they became our favorite ingredient in cooking. In fact, we fell for chiles so hard that between us we've authored thirty books on them and fiery foods, plus produced trade shows and video documentaries, and edited two magazines on the subject of pungent peppers. Considering this chile pepper hang-up of ours, and the fact that we still grill or smoke food every week, it was inevitable that the two biggest loves of our lives (sorry, spouses) would collide in this cataclysmic eruption of fiery heat and smoky flavor that we modestly entitle *Barbecue Inferno*.

We have called for the most authentic chiles possible in the recipes, but since some are not commonly available, we have suggested acceptable substitutes. Also, we have used the same heat levels—mild, medium, hot, and extremely hot—as in our other books. Needless to say, they are approximate. There are no extremely hot dishes in the book.

So, grab some pods from the garden, fire up the smoker, turn on the gas grill, and descend, with Dave and Nancy as your Virgil, into the pit known as the *Barbecue Inferno*. Oh yes, and grab a beer before you go, 'cause it's gonna get hot.

IMPORTANT ADVICE FOR COOKS

Since most of these recipes require some sort of advance preparation, we're not going to remind you about it over and over in the headnotes to the recipes. So don't be surprised to see some long marinating times! In fact, we're not going to nag you about cleaning the grill each time, either.

The cooking times depend on a number of factors, including the heat of your fire, the thickness and moistness of the meat or vegetables, the wind, the humidity, the distance of the food from the fire, and whether or not you use the unit's cover. In each recipe, we give suggested fire or smoke temperature, suggested length of cooking time, suggested internal temperature when possible to measure, and then suggest you cut it open to check it. Just pay attention and you'll be fine. Remember, food on the grill and in the pit is more of an art than a science.

ONE

Outdoor Heat

or,

A Description of the Mechanical Wonders
and Earthy Substances You Will Need to Use This Book

DO YOU WANT a truly authentic barbecue? Well, simply dig a trench in your backyard, fill it with oak logs, and burn them down to coals. Construct a wooden rack for the meat to hang on over the coals, throw on some green wood, and smoke away to your heart's content. That was the way it was done in the old days, and it will still work today. Of course, you won't have much of a lawn left, but at least you can tell all your friends that, by golly, you are an authentic barbecuer. On the other extreme, you can embrace technology and use a state-of-the-art grill with every conceivable feature including instant video replay to catch every exciting moment of that eight-hour smoking of the brisket. Well, almost.

> If flies begin to land on your meat in the smoker, the smoke is definitely not hot enough.
>
> —Anonymous

OF SMOKERS AND BARBECUES

Grillers have many equipment options to choose from—maybe too many. There are table grills, hibachis, kettle grills, steel drum barbecues, built-in grills, Japanese kamados, and literally dozens of models of gas grills. There are nearly as many different kinds of smokers: electric smokers, water smokers, gas smokers, mobile smokers pulled by trucks, and finally, the tried-and-true steel cylinder smoker with attached firebox.

We could spend about twenty-five pages going into excruciating detail about the pros and cons of all these options. Rather than describe every single type of grill and smoker available today, however, we're going to take a shortcut and discuss only the ones you need to prepare the recipes in this book.

Ideally, you should have three pieces of equipment that will enable you to cook with the three main types of fuel: wood, charcoal, and gas. First, the wood smoker. Many books will tell you that you can use a kettle grill to smoke meats—build a fire to the side, let it burn down to coals, place the meat on the grill away from the fire with a pan of water beneath it, sprinkle soaked wood chips over the coals, and *voila*, you are smoking. Just try to keep that little fire going for eight hours! Every time you open the lid to adjust the fire, all the smoke dissipates. Forget it and get a real smoker, one where the firebox is separate and connected by a flue to the main smoking chamber. This allows you to easily keep the fire going without opening the lid to the smoking chamber. Many such smokers have a thermometer on top of the smoking chamber so you can maintain the heat and smoke at precisely the right temperature. Our theory is that if you're serious about smoking, you should use the right tools and not jury-rig grills into smokers. Call us purists, but we feel the same way about gas and electric smokers. Get a real smoker that uses smoldering wood to produce the smoke.

Obviously, we are smoke snobs, but we have to point out that inexpensive water smokers work well for smoking meats that need only a light smoking with plenty of moisture, like chicken and fish. These units come in both electric and charcoal models and are the perfect answer for the home griller who doesn't want to have a 500-pound traditional smoker on the patio.

Charcoal barbecue units range from simple kettles to elaborate units with numerous options. Since you will only be grilling food over hot coals, buy a simple unit with the following features: a lid, adjustable grill, air vents, and, if possible, bottom access to the fuel. If you don't want to buy a charcoal unit, consider a smoker that can double as a charcoal grill. The Oklahoma Joe smoker we use can burn charcoal in the main smoking chamber, but the grill is not adjustable up and down. Also, it's difficult to add fuel during the cooking process because one of the grills must be removed, which means that the meat has to first be moved.

Gas grills are extremely easy to use. An additional benefit is that the dripping fat and meat juices hit the metal bars or lava stones and release aromas that penetrate the meat and give it a barbecue flavor. Depending on the fea-

—*The Expert Pitwoman*—
Today's Topic: It's the Smoke!

Barbecue is smoke, and not too much heat, and plenty of time. You can barbecue less-than-choice cuts. You cannot grill them. It takes low heat to tenderize a brisket. Remember that old physics rule. Water boils at 212 degrees. Boil the water out of a tough piece of meat and what have you got? New sandals.

—Linda West Eckhardt, *The Only Texas Cookbook*

tures you get, a gas grill can cost anywhere from two hundred to a few thousand dollars. We recommend getting one with a built-in thermometer, electric ignition, adjustable heat controls, a rotisserie, and a gas gauge. Some purists insist that gas grills are inferior to charcoal for grilling steaks because they don't produce enough heat, but now there are gas grills that produce 33,000 Btus or more, which is sufficient for steaks. The major problem with gas grills is that they produce maximum temperatures with the cover closed, which means that you are baking the food as much as grilling it. The ideal gas grill produces high temperatures when the cover is open.

HOW HOT IS THAT FIRE, ANYWAY?

You could, of course, use a temperature gauge, but here's a method that will give you a good indication of the fire's heat. Place the palm of your hand four inches above the source of heat and count the number of seconds it takes before you feel uncomfortable and must pull your hand away.

2 seconds: a hot fire, about 375° or more

3 seconds: a medium-hot fire, about 350°

4 seconds: a medium fire, about 300°

5 seconds: a low fire, about 200 to 250°

To cool down after the test, wrap your hand around an ice-cold beer.

TOOLS OF THE BBQ TRADE

There are literally dozens and dozens of toys—oops, make that tools—available for the griller and smoker of the family. Everyone's seen the wacky hats and aprons decorated with pictures of beer cans and whole dead chickens. You can run your credit card up to the limit picking out the gadgets to go with your barbecue unit, but do you really need them all? Since the answer is probably no, we're going to cut to the bone, so to speak, and let you know what you really need for outdoor cooking. We'll start with the assumption that you already have a sharp knife and a cutting board.

TONGS AND SPATULAS

Forget about the long-handled fork, which pierces meats and dries them out too quickly. Always use long-handled tongs to turn meats and vegetables on a grill. Likewise, long-handled spatulas are useful for turning meat patties (not that you'd ever cook an ordinary hamburger).

MITTS

Because your hand may get grilled as you're turning those sixty-four chicken legs, buy an insulated mitt, but make sure that the ends of the mitt fit through the openings in the handles of the tongs. Heavy-duty garden gloves also work fine, but watch out for the dirt. There are also spring-loaded tongs without the holes in the handles, and mitts work fine with them. When moving hunks of smoked meats too large for tongs, switch to neoprene gloves that firefighters use.

INSTANT-READ MEAT THERMOMETER

No need to slice open a chunk of meat to test the doneness. These thermometers have a sharp probe that penetrates the meat and gives you a quick reading of the internal temperature, effectively taking the guesswork out of grilling and smoking.

SKEWERS

Both metal skewers and bamboo or wood skewers work fine, but the former last longer than the latter, which have a tendency to burn. On the other hand, wooden skewers make for a better presentation at the table.

This One's Big Enough for Texas

Bud Liffick of Houston is the owner of the world's largest mobile barbecue pit, which he has named "Cuz." So large that it has to be pulled
by a semi, Cuz is 80 feet long, weighs 90,000 pounds, and has 24 doors,
but only one firebox. At one time it can cook between 700 to 900
briskets, plus a like volume of ribs and chicken. Bud takes Cuz to
major barbecue cook-offs, where cooks have won major prizes by
using it. And how much does a pit like Cuz cost? Bud told us that he
spent $360,000 building it.

VEGETABLE BASKET

We have a sturdy metal basket fashioned from steel mesh that holds about
two cups of sliced vegetables tossed in a little olive oil. Placed directly on the
grill, the basket prevents the loss of vegetable slices that either fall through
the grill or get bumped off it. In a pinch, small aluminum foil roasting pans
with holes poked in the bottom will work fine.

FISH BASKET

This is a hinged apparatus that holds whole fish or fillets so that you don't
have to scrape them off the grill with a spatula. Long handles make them
very easy to turn without damaging the fish, but be sure to use a mitt when
grasping the handles.

BASTING BRUSHES AND MOPS

An inexpensive, two-inch paintbrush works fine for putting basting sauces
on grilled items, and so do the cotton mops that are sold specifically for the
job. Just be sure that the brushes have natural bristles. Nylon bristles will
melt. Most brushes and mops are dishwasher safe.

CHARCOAL CHIMNEY

This is a cylindrical metal tool, open at both ends with legs on the bottom. The bottom is stuffed with crumpled newspapers and charcoal

Preventing Flare-ups

Flare-ups occur when dripping fat ignites on the heat source, enveloping the meat in flames and charring it, ruining its flavor, aroma, texture, and color. The best ways to avoid these embarrassing moments are to:

1. Pay close attention to your fire and your cooking. Don't wander off from the grill to watch the game in the living room.

2. Make sure the fire isn't too hot. Adjust the fire by turning down the gas or raising the grill above the coals.

3. Move the dripping meat away from the hottest coals.

4. Remove the meat immediately when a flare-up begins. You usually have some warning.

5. Keep a spray water bottle handy to wet the coals or douse the flaring meat.

chunks are placed on top of them. When the paper is lit, the chimney effect quickly ignites the charcoal, making petroleum charcoal lighters obsolete. Electric loop starters work well too, though they are a little slower than a chimney.

DRIP PAN

This is an aluminum foil roasting pan that is placed beneath the meat to catch fat, juices, and excess basting sauces when smoking in a charcoal unit.

SPRAY BOTTLE OR SQUIRT GUN

These are the tools to deal with flare-ups.

DRY SPRAY FIRE EXTINGUISHER

This is the tool to use for really big flare-ups, like when you forget to clean the grill and turn your gas burners on high and forget about them for a while.

In addition to these tools, some outdoor cooking experts recommend the following: a refrigerator or cooler for the marinades and beer; a kitchen syringe for injecting bastes directly into the meats; a rotisserie unit for turning roasts and whole fowl; and an electric spice mill for grinding spices used in rubs and sauces.

WOODS FOR GRILLING AND SMOKING

Do we really have to state in print not to use construction lumber scraps in your smoker or barbecue? Well, here we go. Most of these scraps are resinous pine or fir; some, like plywood, are treated or contain glue. All are useless for cooking or smoking purposes. And under no circumstances should you grill or smoke over woods such as cottonwood, willow, pine, or poplar. Stick to the woods listed on the following pages, and you'll produce great heat and fragrant smoke. When you consider smoking foods, think of the wood as a spice to add flavor rather than just a fuel.

The woods that work best for grilling and smoking are hardwoods, particularly (for some unknown reason) the woods of certain fruit and nut trees. We should point out that any of these woods can be used to smoke any meat—we are just mentioning the meats these woods are commonly linked with. Some woods are available locally only where they grow, such as alder and pecan. But most woods are available by mail order or at your nearest barbecue supply store. In most cases, the hard remnants of the fruits and nuts of the hardwood trees can also be used in the smoking process. Specifically, we mean peach pits and nut shells, but not acorns.

- **Alder** imparts a light flavor that works well with fish and poultry. It is native to the northwestern United States and is the traditional wood used for smoking salmon.

- **Apple** has a sweet, mild flavor and is used mostly with pork and game, but can be used for ham as well.

- **Cherry** is also used for ham, but some cooks think that its smoke is too acrid.

- **Hickory,** probably the most famous smoking hardwood, is the wood of choice in the Southern barbecue belt. It imparts a strong, hearty flavor to meats and is used mostly to smoke pork shoulders and ribs.

Herb and Garlic Flavored Smoke

In addition to aromatic hardwoods, various other flavor enhancers can be placed near the coals in the firebox to provide aromatic smoke. Fresh herbs are preferred over rehydrated dried herbs; try bundles of thyme, basil, Mexican oregano, and cilantro tied together. Take care that the herb bundles make smoke rather than burn up immediately. Whole heads of garlic, especially elephant garlic, placed on the coals, add subtle flavors by way of the smoke and vapors produced.

 Maple produces a mild and mellow smoke that imparts a sweet flavor. It is traditionally used for smoking ham but is also good for poultry, pork, and seafood.

 Mesquite is better for grilling than smoking because the smoke tends to be resinous and bitter. Despite all the recent hype about mesquite, few serious barbecuers use it exclusively except for the grill or for in-ground pit barbecues, with their limited amounts of smoke. Mesquite is the strongest flavored wood used in outdoor cooking, and it is popular with restaurant grills that cook meat for a very short time.

 Oak, the favorite wood of Europe, is strong but not overpowering. It is a very good wood for beef or lamb and is probably the most versatile of the hardwoods. Do not use acorns for smoking.

 Pecan is similar to hickory yet milder. It's also a southern favorite and is becoming the smoking wood of choice in the Southwest, where we live, because of the extensive pecan groves in Texas, New Mexico, and Arizona. Because of its availability, it is the wood most commonly used in our smoker.

Remember that the above woods can be mixed in the smoking process to add another dimension to barbecue. Some cooks here in the Southwest mix a little of the stronger mesquite in with pecan or apple wood. Other woods used in the smoking process include almond, black walnut, juniper (slightly resinous), and locust. There are other woods that you can add to the heat source as flavorings, but we don't recommend smoking with them for lengthy periods of time. They produce smoke that is very intensely flavored. If you like the flavor of coconut, for instance, then add a coconut hull to the fire when you smoke or grill fish. Also, grapevines make a tart smoke that can overwhelm poultry or lamb. Use it sparingly. Herbs, such as oregano, sage, thyme, marjoram, rosemary, and basil, used both dried and fresh, can imbue the meat being smoked with their own particular flavor profiles. The thick, woody, stems of rosemary and sage can be used as well as the branches and leaves. As with grapevines, a little goes a long way.

Incidentally, do not burn chile pods to flavor grilled or smoked meat. The pods produce an acrid smoke so irritating that Native Americans burned huge piles of them in an attempt to use gas warfare against the invading Conquistadors. It didn't work with the Conquistadors, but it will ruin your Cornish game hen. Use the chile in the rubs to flavor the meat or in the basting sauce or barbecue sauce you serve on the table. Or maybe in all of them.

To start the wood fire in the smoker's firebox, do not use petroleum-based starters such as a charcoal lighter. They can impart nasty odors. Instead, build the fire in precisely the same way you would in your fireplace: crumpled newspaper, kindling made from thin slivers of the wood you are using, and large pieces of wood on top. Allow the smoker to reach the optimum temperature and make sure the smoke is gray rather than black before you place the meat on the rack or grill for smoking.

THE DARK SIDE OF CHARCOAL—
WITH A NATURAL SOLUTION

Depending on what type of charcoal you buy, you are either getting the perfect, natural fuel for grilling or black lumps made from a slurry composed of sawdust, tree bark, borax, limestone, wood scraps, and a petroleum binder. The former is natural lump charcoal, made by firing logs in a kiln with virtually no air; the latter is the common briquets sold in supermarkets. Sometimes these briquets are further adulterated by being soaked in starter fluids so that they will light when a single match is applied. Some sources defend these briquets by claiming that all the petroleum products are burned off. Yeah, right. Impatient grillers often start the grilling process long before the briquets have burned down to coals, resulting in some intriguing petroleum overtones to the food being grilled. We advise outdoor cooks to avoid all briquets that do not clearly state that they are 100 percent wood.

There are briquets that are pure wood with natural binders—if you can find them. The other charcoal that is excellent is lump charcoal, which tends to burn hot, though a little unevenly. Lump mesquite charcoal is excellent and even superior in some ways to the wood itself because most of the resins have evaporated. In fact, lump charcoal can be used in the firebox of the smoker if green wood or soaked hardwood chips are added to produce the smoke.

After choosing your charcoal, do not use any petroleum-based lighter fluids to start the fire. Use a charcoal chimney, (see page 5) readily available at stores stocking grilling accessories. Lighting the crumpled-up newspapers at the bottom provides enough heat to start the charcoal. Another solution is an electric starter, which works very well and very quickly.

CALL IT SMOKE-GRILLING

The Jamaican jerk cooks have perfected a technique for cooking pork and chicken that combines the best elements of grilling and smoking. The meat is cooked directly over pimento wood (allspice) coals, but the grills are about fifteen inches above the heat. Smoke is produced by adding green pimento leaves and stems to the coals. Corrugated aluminum is placed directly on top of the meat to catch and retain the smoke.

For cooks who like just a little smoke to their meats, this technique is easily duplicated in both charcoal and gas grills. In a charcoal grill, simply add soaked hardwood chips to the coals and close the lid for a few minutes in the early stages of cooking. With practice, the cook will learn how long to smoke-grill various meats with various woods. This technique is a little trickier with a gas grill. Some have special boxes where you can add wood chips. If yours doesn't, you can put the dry wood chips in a metal pan and place it on the grill next to the meat. Remember, this is not true smoking over low heat—but it does work, and we defy any grill or smoke proponent to produce better pork than that at the Double-V Jerk Center in Ocho Rios, Jamaica, where we learned the smoke-grilling technique.

STOVE-TOP SMOKING

Sure it's heresy to smoke meats indoors, but it can be done. Now there are stainless steel stove-top smokers on the market that resemble a deep roasting pan. They have a rack, a drip pan, and a cover that keeps the smoke in the unit. "Smoke dust," or very fine chips of wood, produce the smoke from the very bottom of the pan. These units are great for people who live in apartments and don't have space for a regular outdoor smoker. Although it's difficult to smoke large pieces of meat, these smokers are great for small pieces of fish or chicken.

You can also use a wok or Dutch oven for smoking, provided that you have a tight-fitting lid to keep the smoke inside. You line the wok with aluminum foil and place the smoking mixture—very fine wood chips—on the foil. Place the meat on a cake rack about three inches above the smoking mixture. Turn the heat to high, cover the unit, and just in case, disconnect your house smoke detector. Decrease the heat to medium and continue to smoke according to the recipe. You will need to add more wood chips from time to time.

GETTING THE CRUD OFF THE GRILL

In both the grilling and smoking processes, organic material will accumulate on the grills—fat, pieces of meat, basting sauces, dead moths. Known in the barbecue industry technically as crud, this stuff will quickly burn and fuse to the metal. Since you always want to start cooking with a clean grill, this crud poses a problem, especially for the lazy cleaner. Some people simply place the grill as close as possible to the hottest flame and allow the accumulated material to turn to ash, which they then wipe off with paper towels. Well, not only are they risking a fire if the crud has a lot of fat in it, but the crud rarely carbonizes completely. Many cooks will then use a wire brush to get right down to the metal. This works fine, but it is labor intensive and sweaty going.

The easiest way to clean a grill is to remove it from the unit, spray it thoroughly front and back with oven cleaner, and place it in a plastic trash bag, which you tie shut. Allow it to marinate overnight, then rinse it off with a hose the next day.

HOW TO BE SURE WHEN IT'S DONE

Note from Dave: I have been roasting, grilling, and smoking meats for nearly a half century, and I never used a thermometer of any kind until this year (1999). I remained in the old school of cooking, knowing the general rules of how many minutes per pound of meat should cook at a given temperature. When the time was up, or when instinct told me the grilled meat was ready, I performed my test: I cut the darned thing open and looked at it. This year, I bought a digital instant-read thermometer, and I have to say that it works fine. It was a little slow on the read-out (wear gloves or a mitt when inserting), but after a few seconds I knew precisely what the temperature was. But then, I sliced the meat and found it too rare. Why? I think internal temperatures of meat when done vary according to muscling, marbling, aging, bones, and the actual composition of the meat depending on what the animal ate—grain versus grass, for example. Here's the deal: Thermometers are an indicator, not a guarantee of success. Use them to check on the meat, but if you have any doubts, probe the meat. If juices flow, it is undercooked. Likewise if the fish doesn't flake, it's not done yet.

Use the following charts along with an instant-read meat thermometer to gauge when the meat is finished to the desired doneness. Make sure that the probe doesn't touch any bones; they conduct heat and will give a different reading. It is extremely difficult to measure fish temperatures—Nancy claims impossible—so the probes work best only on thick fish steaks. And it's very difficult to measure the temperature of ribs and kebabs, so rely on instinct and cutting into the meat to check the doneness.

	rare	medium rare	medium	well done
PORK	—	—	160°	175°
POULTRY	—	—	160°	175°
BEEF AND LAMB	140°	150°	160°	170°
FISH		*done at 135°*		

GRILLING AND THE "C" WORD

Since everything we love to ingest is bad for us these days, it should come as no surprise that the experts are busy linking grilling and smoking to cancer. Grilling and smoking pollute the air (is that an odor or a fragrance?), so we outdoor cooks are inhaling not only vegetable smoke (from wood or charcoal) but also smoke and chemicals in the charcoal additives, in the propane, or in the charcoal lighter. And that's just the tip of the briquet. The grilling of meat, poultry, and fish has been linked to heterocyclic amines (HCAs) and benzopyrene, and both have caused tumors in laboratory animals. The food police, animal rights groups, and vegans were dancing in the streets over these revelations for a while, but now the controversy has—uh, cooled down a bit.

When we studied some of these reports, we found an amazing number of weasel words but no real proof of anything. *The American Institute for Cancer Research Newsletter* used the words "suspected to promote cancer," and "research has linked HCAs to cancer." The link must be tenuous because to our knowledge, no cause-and-effect relationship between grilled meats and cancer has ever been proven, and, amazingly enough, no government agency has ever recommended eliminating grilling and smoking as cooking methods.

However, being the caring health nuts that we are, here are some directives for ultra-responsible grilling:

🌿 Remove excess fat and/or skin from meat and poultry before grilling.

🌿 Use the indirect grilling method for cooking high-fat foods (smoking also works well).

🌿 Do not burn or blacken the meat, though the latter is hard to prevent when smoking brisket. (Okay, give the burnt ends to your worst enemy.)

🌿 Avoid contact between the meat and the flames, and, obviously, don't allow flare-ups to occur.

🌿 Marinating the meat for even a few minutes reduces HCA formation when the meat is grilled.

TWO

Chiles on the Grill

Roast 'em, Peel 'em, Smoke 'em, and then Cook with 'em

ALTHOUGH MANY different fruits and vegetables can be grilled or smoked, it is chile peppers that have a particular affinity for the open flame. Fire leads to two important techniques for preserving chiles: roasting and peeling or smoking. Blistering or roasting the chile is the process of heating it until the tough transparent skin separates from the meat of the pod and can be removed. Virtually any fresh chile can be roasted and peeled to remove the skin, but generally speaking, the larger the chile, the tougher the skin, so the chiles most commonly roasted are the size of jalapeños or larger. Poblano chiles, *chilacas* (fresh pasillas), and the New Mexican varieties that are harvested green must be roasted and peeled before using them in a recipe. The method is quite simple.

ROASTING AND PEELING TECHNIQUES

While processing the chiles, be sure to wear rubber gloves to protect yourself from the capsaicin that can burn your hands and any other part of your body that it touches. Before roasting, cut a small slit in the chiles close to the top so that the steam can escape. Otherwise, the chiles can literally explode, ruining them for use in anything other than a stew.

Our favorite roasting method is to place the pods on the grill over a charcoal or gas fire about five to six inches from the coals. The pods will soon blister, indicating that the skin is separating. With tongs, turn the pods to ensure that they are blistered all over or they will not peel properly. Sometimes the chile pods will blacken slightly. This does not affect the taste as the blackening is on the skin, which will soon be removed. When roasting the chiles, stand upwind and be careful of the smoke: It can burn the eyes.

When the pods are thoroughly blistered, remove them with tongs and immediately wrap them in damp towels or place them in a plastic bag with damp paper towels for ten to fifteen minutes—this "steams" them and loosens the skins. For crisper, less cooked chiles, remove the pods from the grill with tongs and immediately plunge them into ice water to stop the cooking process. If properly blistered, the tough skin can easily be removed from the pod. The seeds are usually removed, but leave the stem on if you will be making stuffed chiles. At this point, the chiles can be prepared for use in the recipe or preserved by freezing.

Choose the form you want the chiles in—whole, in strips, or chopped. A handy way to put up chopped or diced chiles is to freeze them in plastic trays by making chile ice cubes. When frozen, they can be "popped" out of the trays and stored in a sealable plastic bag in the freezer. When making a soup or a stew, just drop in a cube. This eliminates the problems inherent in hacking apart a large slab of frozen chiles when you need just a couple of ounces.

Roasted and peeled green chiles can also be dried. String the chiles together, cover with cheesecloth and dry in a well-ventilated location. One ounce of this chile *pasado* (dried green chile) is equivalent to about ten fresh chile pods. Excess chile peppers can also be pickled or made into vinegars, oils, pastes, salsas, and sauces.

GRILLING CHILES FOR SALSA

In northern Mexico, one of the favorite methods for making salsa involves grilling chiles and tomatoes. The main difference between this method and the one described above are that the chiles are blackened more and skins are not removed. The blackened bits of skin are actually desirable. To make a simple but splendid grilled salsa such as *Salsa de Jalapeño* or *Serrano Asado* (Grilled Jalapeño or Serrano Salsa), simply grill two large tomatoes on the grate until charred but not too badly burned, turning often. Do the same with two jalapeños or three serranos, stemmed. Place the tomatoes and chiles in a blender with ¼ teaspoon salt and process for thirty seconds. Strain into a serving bowl and serve with chips or over grilled meat or poultry. Variations include adding finely chopped onions and/or minced cilantro after blending.

Fiery Flavors

Chef Mark Miller of the Coyote Café in Santa Fe has assembled a list of forty-one "Chile Flavor Descriptors," which are divided into the categories of "fruity" and "other" flavors. The fruity flavors included citrusy (particularly orange and lemon), which would apply to most varieties of habaneros and some of the yellow South American ajís, and raisin, which is the ever-present aroma of the anchos and pasillas. Other fruity descriptors were black cherry, fig, mango, and melon. In the other flavors category, Miller lists chocolate, tobacco, tannic, soapy, green tea, and—how ironic—black pepper. Unfortunately, the science of chile flavors is still in its infancy, and most of the hundreds of chile varieties have not yet been matched to their flavor descriptors. Undoubtedly, chile chefs on the cutting edge will certainly do more research into this important facet of chile flavor.

DEFINING THE SMOKED CHILES

Generally speaking, the term *chipotle* in English refers to any smoked chile pepper. Although any variety of chile can be smoked, the most commonly smoked chiles are mature, red jalapeños, named for the city of Jalapa in the state of Veracruz, Mexico. Smoked chiles had their origin in the ancient civilization of Teotihuacán, north of present-day Mexico City. It was the largest city-state in Mesoamerica and flourished centuries before the rise of the Aztecs. Chipotles also made an appearance in the marketplaces of Tenochtitlán, the capital city of the Aztecs that is now called Mexico City. Certain varieties of chiles that we now call jalapeños would not dry properly in the sun—their thick flesh would rot first. However, like meats, they could be preserved by the process known as smoke-drying.

The true chipotle, usually called *típico,* is grayish tan, quite stiff, and is often described as looking like a cigar butt. It is deeply imbued with smoke and is both hot and flavorful. Other varieties of smoked jalapeños are often mistaken for the *típico* chipotle. The most common one is called *morita,* which means "little blackberry" in Spanish. The color of this smoked chile is

---

—A Brief History—
The First 400 Years of American Barbecue, Part 2

Real barbecue is one of the most delicious foods ever devised by humankind. But it takes on varying forms and shapes. In Memphis, a pork barbecue sandwich consists of pulled (or pulled and then chopped) shoulder on a hamburger bun, doused with a tomato-based sauce that is tangy, mildly sweet, and barely piquant—and topped with a scoop of coleslaw. In Kentucky, pork becomes mutton. In North Carolina, the mild tanginess of Tennessee becomes the powerful force of vinegar, and in South Carolina the tomato-based sauce is replaced by mustard. Drive 100 miles into Missouri, and the whole pork shoulder yields to the smaller butt portion. If you travel further west than Arkansas, pork gives way to beef and poultry.

—Jeffrey Steingarten, "Going Whole Hog"

---

dark red, sometimes approaching purple in color. Often the *morita* is referred to as smoked serrano chile, but this is inaccurate. Both the *típico* and the *morita* are smoked jalapeños; the difference being that the *morita* is not smoked nearly as long and thus remains very leathery and pliable. Not only is the smoky flavor much more intense in the *típico*, its flavor is much richer.

Other varieties of smoked chiles include:

🌿 *Cobán*: a piquín chile that is smoked in southern Mexico and Guatemala.

🌿 *Pasilla de Oaxaca*: a variety of chile that is smoked in Oaxaca and is used in the famous *mole negro*.

🌿 *Jalapeño chico*: jalapeños that are smoked while still green. Usually, they are culls from the market that need to be preserved rather than thrown away, and the smoke-drying process obscures any blemishes.

🌿 *Capones*: rare smoked chiles that are a red jalapeño without seeds. The term means "castrated ones." They are quite expensive and are rarely exported.

The Chilehead on BBQ

Francis X. Tolbert, the famous chile expert, covers Mexican food and barbecue in his book, *A Bowl of Red*. In his discussion of King Solomon, one of east Texas's most memorable barbecue artists, Tolbert observes: "He believed that his success at barbecuing rested heavily on his 'secret devil's sauce,' and he wouldn't tell anyone, not even his family, the formula, although some of the ingredients were, obviously, fresh chile pepper sauce, Worcestershire sauce (King Solomon made his own Worcestershire), black pepper, and vinegar. It was very hot."

🌢 *Habanero*: a smoked habanero product that has been introduced recently in the United States. It is used as a very hot substitute for chipotles.

The heat scales of chipotles vary considerably. The *coban* and habaneros are the hottest of the smoked chiles and the *morita* and *típico* are the mildest. Since jalapeños have medium heat, when smoked they retain the same heat level, which ranges from about 5,000 to 10,000 Scoville Units (see page vi), measured in the dried form. By comparison, poblanos and New Mexican chiles are typically 500 to 1,000 Scoville Units, and habaneros range from 80,000 to more than 300,000 Scoville Units. When many chipotles are added to a dish, the result can be quite pungent.

SMOKING TECHNIQUES

In the town of Delicias in northern Mexico, large batches of red jalapeños are smoked in a large underground pit on a rack made of wood, bamboo, or metal. Another nearby pit contains the fire and is connected to the smoking pit by a tunnel. The pods are placed on top of the rack in the first pit where drafts of air pull the smoke from the second pit up and over the pods. A chile farm may have a smoker of a different design at the edge of the fields: It may be a fireplace of bricks with grates at the top and a firebox below. This smoker is used for smaller batches than the underground pits.

Chipotles smoked in the Mexican manner are not always available north of Mexico. And with the price topping $15.00 per pound when they are available, an attractive alternative is for cooks to smoke their own chiles. There are five keys to the quality of the homemade chipotles: the maturity and quality of the pods, the moisture in the pods, the type of wood used to create the smoke, the temperature of the smoke drying the pods, and the amount of time the fruits are exposed to the smoke and heat. But remember that smoking is an art, so variations are to be expected and even desired.

Our Favorite Barbecue Cook-Off Teams' Names

Great Boars of Fire

Super Swine Swizzlers

Hazardous Waist

Pork, Sweat & Tears

Seven Basted Bubbas

The Smoke-A-Holics

Ideally, you should use a smoker that is dedicated solely to chiles, but this is impractical. If you use your meat smoker, be sure to clean the grate thoroughly first.

Recommended woods for smoking chiles are fruit trees or other hardwoods such as hickory, oak, and pecan. Pecan is used extensively in parts of Mexico and in southern New Mexico to flavor chipotle. Although mesquite is a smoke source in Mexico, we prefer the less resinous hardwoods. Mesquite charcoal (not briquets) is acceptable, especially when soaked hardwood chips are placed on top of the coals to create even more smoke. It is possible, however, that the resinous mesquite smoke (from the wood, not charcoal) contributes to the tan-brown coloration of the *típico* variety of chipotle.

Wash all the pods and discard any that have insect damage, bruises, or are soft, then remove the stems from the pods. Place the whole red jalapeños on the grate as close together as possible. Depending on the amount of moisture in the jalapeños, the thickness of the flesh, the humidity in the smoke, and the heat of the smoke, the entire process can take anywhere from twenty-four to forty-eight hours. The result will look more like the *morita* than the *típico*. For some unknown reason, it is very difficult to duplicate the color and stiffness of the *típico* chipotle. Obviously, the Mexicans have perfected the *típico* technique, while we Americans are struggling to duplicate it with more modern equipment. There is a delicate balance between the pit temperature, the amount of smoke, the type of

A Winning Rib-Smoking Technique

This application of smoke won first place for ribs in the 1992 Memphis in May competition for the Apple City BBQ Team of Murphysboro, Tennessee.

🌿 Preliminary: The ribs are rubbed with a secret combination of sixteen spices.

🌿 Hour 1: The ribs are smoked at a temperature of 100°F.

🌿 Hour 2: The temperature of the smoke increases to 180 to 200°F and the ribs are basted with fresh apple juice twice.

🌿 Hour 3: The temperature increases to 250°F and the ribs are basted with apple juice twice more.

🌿 Hour 4: Two light coatings of a secret finishing sauce are applied, and then more of the spice rub is sprinkled over all. Smoke at 250° for 30 more minutes, making the total smoking time 3½ hours.

smoke, and the length of time needed to produce the perfect chipotle. Perhaps we shall be forced to dig smoking pits in our backyards and begin growing mesquite trees.

You can also make chipotles in a Weber-type barbecue unit with a lid. The grate should be thoroughly cleaned to remove any meat particles because any odor in the unit will give the chipotles an undesirable flavor. Again, the result of this type of smoking is a chipotle that more resembles the red *morita* than the classic grayish tan *típico*.

Start two small fires on either side of the barbecue bowl, preferably using one of the recommended hardwoods. Place the pods in a single layer on the grill rack so they fit between the two fires. For quicker smoking, cut the pods in half lengthwise and remove the seeds. Keep the fires small and never directly expose the pods to the fire so they won't dry unevenly or burn. The intention is to dry the pods slowly while flavoring them with smoke. If you are using charcoal, soak hardwood chips in water before placing them on the coals so the wood will burn slower and create more smoke. The barbecue vents should be opened only partially to allow a small amount of air to enter the barbecue, thus preventing the fires from burning too fast and creating too much heat.

Check the pods, the fires, and the chips hourly and move the pods around, always keeping them away from the fire. It may take up to forty-eight hours to dry the pods completely, which means that your fires will probably burn down during the night and will need to be restoked in the morning. When dried properly, the pods will be hard, light in weight, and dark red or brown in color. After the pods have dried, remove them from the grill and let them cool. To preserve their flavor, place them in a sealable plastic bag.

Ten pounds of fresh jalapeños yield just one pound of chipotles after the smoking process is complete. A pound of chipotles goes a long way: A single pod is usually enough to flavor a dish.

A quick smoking technique involves drying red jalapeños (sliced lengthwise, seeds removed) in a dehydrator or in an oven with just the pilot light on. They should be desiccated but not stiff. Next, smoke them for three hours over fruitwood in a traditional smoker with a separate firebox, or in the Weber-style barbecue as described above. This technique separates the drying from the smoking so you spend less time fueling the smoker.

Other varieties of chiles can be smoked as well, and because they are less fleshy, it takes less time. For example, habaneros generally can be smoked in about half the time as jalapeños. Even dried pods, such as the red New Mexican varieties, can be smoked for a few hours to add a smoky dimension to their already fine flavor.

STORING CHIPOTLES AND MAKING POWDER

Many cooks have success storing chipotles in a sealable plastic bag in a cool and dry location. If humidity is kept out of the bag, the chipotle will keep for twelve to twenty-four months. A more secure method for storing them at room temperature is to keep them in glass jars with tight-fitting, rubber-sealed tops. Of course, the best storage of all is to freeze them. Use heavy-duty freezer bags and double-bag them. They will keep for years with no noticeable loss of flavor or smoke.

Defining Barbecue

Primitive summertime rite at which spirits are present, hunks of meat are sacrificed by being burnt on braziers by sauce-smeared men wearing old hat and aprons with cabalistic slogans, and human flesh is offered to insects.

—Henry Beard and Roy McKie, *Cooking: A Cook's Dictionary*

True barbecue, let me explain, is meat slow-roasted over wood at a low enough temperature to lose about a third of its weight in moisture during the cooking process.

—John Thorne, "Serious Pig"

A "dried" chipotle usually has about 80 to 90 percent of its moisture removed, which is enough, with the smoke, to preserve it and retard bacterial growth, but not enough to create a powder. Therefore, regardless of whether you are using the *típico* chipotle or the *morita*, they must be further dried in a food dehydrator or in the oven on the lowest possible heat, until they are so dry that you can snap them in half.

Put on a painter's mask to protect yourself from uncontrollable sneezing, and break the chipotles into manageable pieces. Use an electric spice mill or a coffee grinder to reduce the pod pieces to a powder of the desired consistency.

Because it is so desiccated, the chipotle powder stores well in airtight containers such as small jars. But remember, powders will oxidize and absorb odors from the air or the freezer, so if you intend to freeze the powders or store them in bags at room temperature, triple-bag them first.

OTHER CHILE POWDERS USED IN GRILLING AND SMOKING

All chiles can be dried and ground into powder—and most are, including the habanero. Crushed chiles, or those coarsely ground with some of the seeds, are called *quebrado*. Coarse powders are referred to as *caribe*, while the finer powders are termed *molido*. The milder powders, such as New Mexican, can also be used as the base for sauces, but the hotter powders such as cayenne and piquín are used when heat is needed more than flavor. In our homes, we actually have more powders available than the whole pods because the powders are concentrated and take up less storage space. We store them in small, airtight bottles. The fresher the powders, the better they taste, so don't grind up too many pods. Use an electric spice mill and be sure to wear a painter's mask to protect the nose and throat from the pungent powder. The colors of the powders vary from a bright, electric red-orange (*chiltepíns*), to light green (dried jalapeños), to a dark brown that verges on black (ancho). We love to experiment by changing the powders called for in recipes.

AN ASTOUNDING VARIETY OF COMMERCIAL CHILE PRODUCTS

A vast number of condiments used in the entire barbecue experience now contain chile peppers. There are also myriads of hot sauces and salsas, which can be used as handy substitutes for fresh or dried chiles in recipes. Also, look for chile-infused vinegars, oils, mustards, ketchup, cheeses, pickles, hot sauces, salad dressings, jams and jellies, soups, pastas, potato and corn chips, curry powders and pastes, nuts, and even candies. We're not suggesting that you make your entire barbecue menu hot and spicy, mind you—but then again, why not?

THREE

Aye, There's the Rub

Not to Mention Mops and Sops,
Sauces and Salsas, Marinades, and a Grill Sauce or Two

MEAT THAT IS TO BE GRILLED or smoked is often treated with spice mixtures and marinades of various types before, during, and after the cooking process. In the contentious world of barbecue, there is a great debate not only about which of these marinades to use, but whether or not to use them in the first place. Many grillers, for example, would never use a rub on their sirloin steak. And you'll hear it time and time again from the smoking purists: Good barbecue doesn't need condiments. No rubs, no marinades, no sops, no sauces. If that's so, please tell us why nearly every recipe you can find for Texas barbecued brisket contains at least two of the three following steps:

🌿 Massage a rub into the meat and let stand for ½ hour before smoking.

🌿 Apply a sop during the smoking process.

🌿 Serve the sliced meat topped with a barbecue sauce.

In some recipes, the sliced meat is mixed with the barbecue sauce and allowed to sit before serving. In other recipes, the meat sits in the sop and barbecue sauces are omitted. Some barbecuers prefer just to use a rub, claiming that brisket and ribs get a better crust than when a sop is used. It begins to look as if we are talking here about personal preference. Feel free to omit, add, or adjust any ingredients or techniques in this book. Cooking is more of an art than an exact science, which is why, at any given time, there are tens of thousands of cookbooks to be found with millions of recipes!

Saucing Suggestions

🐾 Serve all barbecue sauces at room temperature.

🐾 Never serve barbecue sauce in a silver gravy boat.

🐾 Do not apply barbecue sauce while the meat is still on the grill or in the pit.

🐾 At the table, wear sauce protection at all times—a bib with a pig on it.

🐾 All barbecue and hot sauces, commercial or homemade, should be refrigerated after use. The higher the vinegar content, the longer they will last in the refrigerator—which is months for most commercial sauces.

Let's examine the various spicing and saucing techniques in order of use.

RUBBING IT THE RIGHT WAY

Rubs are essentially dry spice mixtures. A rub can be as simple as crushed black pepper, or as elaborate as a jerk or curry rub. Their purpose is to add intense flavor to the meat without adding excessive moisture. A paste is a rub with a little moisture—usually water, beer, or oil—added to bind it. Generally speaking, rubs are used more with meat and poultry and pastes more with seafood. A notable exception to this rule is Jamaican jerk pork, which can be treated with either a jerk rub, a jerk paste, or in some cases (mostly outside Jamaica), a jerk sauce.

The most important thing to remember about making rubs is to use the freshest possible ingredients, not the ground oregano that's been in your cupboard since 1986. Older spices and herbs oxidize, or turn rancid, and either lose flavor or gain a flavor you don't want on your meat. Buy spices such as mustard, black pepper, cumin, and coriander in whole form and

Make Great BBQ Sauce

Barbecue expert Brother Mel Johnson suggests the following proce-
dures when creating your own signature sauce.

🌿 Start with a commercial sauce and doctor it up with chile peppers
or other ingredients that you like.

🌿 If you are intent on creating your own, begin with the best grade
ketchup you can buy.

🌿 Slow-cook the sauce at a low temperature.

🌿 Use a mixture of spices that you like.

🌿 Make a sauce that has a good balance of sweet and hot. That way,
it will please almost everyone.

grind them yourself. The same goes for chile peppers—buy the pods, not
the powder. Spices should preferably be fresh, but we've bought some
incredible dried Mexican oregano in bulk. Dry fresh spices in the microwave and then crush them in a mortar.

You can use a spice mill, a coffee grinder, or a mortar and pestle to make
the rubs, just remember not to grind the mixture too finely. The friction
and heat of the grinder motor can make the herbs and spices release too
much of their essential oils.

Rubs—and particularly pastes—do not store very well. If you must
store a rub, put it in a small jar with a tight seal and place it in a cool, dry
cupboard, or in the freezer. Oxygen and light are the enemies of a rub.
Pastes can be stored for a few days, though only in the refrigerator.

Dry rubs are massaged into the meat or poultry, which is then lightly covered and allowed to sit for as little as a half hour, or as long as a day. When
using pastes on seafood, completely cover the shrimp or fish or whatever
with the paste, then wrap tightly in plastic wrap to more fully infuse it with
flavor. The same technique works with pastes applied to meat or poultry.

Debates continue to rage about the use of rubs in the barbecue process.

Some people state that the rub seals the meat, keeping the juices in, but others warn that salt in the rub will draw the juices out, and they will evaporate. (Note that most rubs have a little salt in them.) At least one home physicist theorizes that the dryness of the rub attracts moisture from the air and actually adds it to the meat, but this is doubtful. Barbecue writer Richard Langer explains that "a rub draws a portion of the juices from a cut of meat to the surface, there to mingle with the seasoning and form a crust encasing the rest of the meat's juices and flavors."

Ha! Food chemistry expert Harold McGee counters: "Any crust that forms around the surface of the meat is not waterproof." In the end it seems that if we use food common sense and don't add additional salt before smoking and don't worry about moisture loss—smoked meats are *supposed* to lose moisture as they tenderize—we can assume that rubs add flavor and help make a tasty crust, or burnt ends, as the barbecuers call the crust on the thin end of the brisket.

A MYRIAD OF MARINADES

A marinade is a liquid mixture used to soak meats of all kinds before they are grilled. Many experts recommend not marinating meats that are to be smoked. A case could be made that applying sops during the smoking process is the same thing as marinating the meat. But applying a thin sauce to a meat that is smoking is a different process than a lengthy soaking that can break down the muscle fibers.

"Marinades containing wine or vinegar can also tenderize the surface of the meat—their acid denatures the surface proteins—but again the result will be drier meat," writes chemistry expert Harold McGee, who noted that such acidic materials don't penetrate far enough into the meat for tenderizing purposes. But marinades are more than just meat tenderizers—they add an enormous amount of flavor to grilled meats. Except those containing wine and vinegar, they can even add moisture to drier cuts of meat. Howard Hillman in *Kitchen Science* agrees and notes that this occurs even when using acidic marinades. "However, on balance, the marinated meat's juice loss is usually more than compensated by a gain in tenderness and flavor."

The permutations and combinations of ingredients in a marinade sometimes seem infinite. In basic form, however, they usually combine an oil of

The Other Side of Sauces

Here's what barbecue sauce cannot do for you:

🌿 Convert bad barbecue into good barbecue: If the barbecue is bad, throw it out!

🌿 Erase wrinkles. It can please your palate, but it's not a wonder drug.

🌿 Substitute fake barbecue for real barbecue. The secret to some barbecue may be in the sauce, but if the meat hasn't been cooked with the direct action of fire and smoke, it isn't barbecue.

—Ardie Davis, *The Great Barbecue Sauce Book*

some sort, an acidic component such as vinegar or citrus juice, and flavorings that range from garlic to habanero chiles, from rosemary to allspice.

You can use large bowls for marinating the meat, but it's handier and takes up less space to use sealable plastic bags, which actually require less marinade to cover the meat. The length of marinating time varies from cook to cook and recipe to recipe, but the softer the meat, the less the marinating time. Fish, poultry, and meat are in order from least to most marinating time.

If you intend to use the same marinade that you've soaked the meat in as a sop or sauce, remember to boil it for a couple of minutes or simmer it for twenty minutes to kill any bacteria released by the uncooked meat.

THE SOP: MARINADE, BASTE, OR BOTH?

A sop, sometimes called mop, is a thin basting sauce that is applied during the smoking process. It keeps the meat moist and adds flavor. Most mops do not contain sugar or tomatoes, because these ingredients will caramelize and the resulting sugars burn easily, even under smoking temperatures. Barbecue expert C. Clark "Smokey" Hale once wrote that the sop is the greatest secret of barbecue, so powerful that it could make "a pine knot tender and delicious." Just remember to keep the sop simmering during the smoking process to avoid breeding bacteria. In the grilling world, a sop is called a grill sauce and is used for basting and generating smoke. Like sops, grill sauces are never sweet so that the meat does not blacken. You can mop or sop your meat with a one- or two-inch-wide paint brush, but the traditional tool is a miniature cotton mop that is available from barbecue supply stores.

FINISHING SAUCES OR JUST PLAIN FINISHED?

"Strictly in terms of flavor, good barbecue needs no saucing at all," claims John Thorne, in his article "Serious Pig." Trying to prove that a true "barbecuist" vandalizes someone else's sauce and improves upon it, rather than creates one from scratch, he goes on to say that "knowing this is what separates the real barbecuist from the dilettante: where for the latter the sauce is everything, for the former it is only a signature of a poem already written."

Even barbecue dilettantes know a good rib when they taste it, and saucing or not is merely a matter of personal preference. Since there are dozens of regional U.S.A. barbecue sauce variations and hundreds of commercial barbecue sauces available, even a "barbecuist" would eventually have to succumb to the tasty lure of one of them.

To sum up, the sauce is not the be-all and end-all of the barbecue process, but it adds moisture and a complementary flavor to the smoked meat. If you are having a barbecue party and a "barbecuist" shows up, serve the barbecue sauce on the side and let him or her make up their own minds. In fact, serve everyone two or three sauces on the side and prove how sauces can brighten up a barbecue. As far as altering existing commercial barbecue sauces for your own nefarious purposes, why not? Barbecue industry surveys indicate that 50 percent of all people who buy a commercial sauce alter it in some way, mostly by adding chile peppers or bottled hot sauce. This is not to mention all the restaurants that use spiced-up versions of national brands that they buy by the keg. Just think of the possibilities of combining your favorite commercial barbecue sauce with your favorite habanero hot sauce! And with the numbers of different barbecue and hot sauces available, the combinations are nearly endless.

Ragin' Cajun Rub

MAKES: 2½ tablespoons
HEAT SCALE: Medium

Here's a concentrated rub that has its origins in Louisiana, where it seems that every home cook has a secret spice mixture for grilled foods. This rub works well with fish and especially shrimp. Sprinkle it on the seafood and allow it to marinate at room temperature for about an hour. It's also good on chicken before it's grilled.

1 tablespoon paprika
2 teaspoons ground cayenne chile
2 teaspoons garlic powder
1 teaspoon freshly ground black
    pepper
1 teaspoon dried thyme
1 teaspoon dried oregano

1 teaspoon onion powder
1 teaspoon salt
1 bay leaf, stemmed and crushed
½ teaspoon ground allspice
¼ teaspoon freshly ground white
    pepper

Combine all the ingredients in a spice grinder and process until finely ground. Store any unused rub in a sealed container in the freezer.

 # Memphis Rib Rub

MAKES: approximately ⅔ cup
HEAT SCALE: Medium

This rub is great for smoking any cut of pork—ribs, chops, steaks, or even a roast. It has its origins in one of the barbecue centers of America, Memphis, Tennessee, home of the Memphis-in-May Barbecue Cook-Off. You can also use rubs on grilled meats, so the next time you grill pork (or lamb) chops, try this rub.

¼ cup paprika

2 tablespoons garlic salt

1 tablespoon freshly ground black
  pepper

2 tablespoons brown sugar

1 tablespoon onion powder

1 tablespoon dried oregano

1 tablespoon dry mustard

1½ teaspoons ground cayenne chile

Combine all the ingredients in a bowl and mix well. Store any unused rub in a sealed container in the freezer.

Jamaican Jerk Dry Rub

MAKES: approximately ½ cup

HEAT SCALE: Hot

Jamaican jerk barbecue is a fine art. When Dave visited a jerk center in Ocho Rios, the jerkmaster told him that the secret was in the spices—the rub that gives the pork and chicken such an intensely spicy-hot flavor. Most Jamaican jerk cooks use a dry rub, but on occasion, and especially for fish or poultry, the rub is transformed into a paste or marinade by adding vegetable oil. You can also sprinkle this rub over steamed or grilled vegetables.

2 tablespoons onion powder

1 tablespoon ground allspice

1 tablespoon ground thyme

2 teaspoons ground cinnamon

2 teaspoons ground cloves

2 teaspoons brown sugar

1 teaspoon garlic powder

2 teaspoons ground dried habanero
  chile

1 teaspoon freshly ground black
  pepper

1 teaspoon ground coriander

½ teaspoon ground nutmeg

½ teaspoon salt

Combine all the ingredients in a bowl and mix well. Store any unused rub in a sealed container in the freezer.

Kansas City Dry Rub

MAKES: ⅔ cup
HEAT SCALE: Medium

From another center of the barbecue universe comes one of the dry rubs that made the American Royal Cook-Off in Kansas City such a highly competitive event. Try this rub on turkey and chicken too.

2 tablespoons brown sugar
2 tablespoons ground paprika
1 tablespoon white sugar
1 tablespoon garlic salt
1 tablespoon celery salt
1 teaspoon ground cayenne chile

1 tablespoon commercial chili
   powder
2 teaspoons freshly ground black
   pepper
½ teaspoon dry mustard

Combine all the ingredients in a bowl and mix well. Store any unused rub in a sealed container in the freezer.

 # Genuine, Authentic South-of-the-Border Chile Rub

MAKES: approximately ⅔ cup
HEAT SCALE: Hot

Yeah, right. Okay, this is our spin on Mexican flavorings that would work on goat, as in cabrito *pit-roasted goat. Can't find goat at your local Wynn-Dixie or Safeway? Use this rub for either grilling or smoking beef, pork, and lamb.*

3 tablespoons ground ancho chile
2 teaspoons ground chile de árbol
2 teaspoons ground chipotle chile
1 teaspoon ground cumin

2 teaspoons dried Mexican or other
   oregano
2 teaspoons onion salt
1 teaspoon garlic powder

Combine all the ingredients in a bowl and mix well. Store any unused rub in a sealed container in the freezer.

Brisket Basting Sauce

MAKES: approximately 5 cups
HEAT SCALE: Medium

This recipe is from Red Caldwell, who revealed the secrets of Texas barbecue to us when we were editors of Chile Pepper *magazine. After a beef brisket has been smoked, it is basted in this sauce for a couple of hours before it is sliced and served. Some cooks slather the sauce on during the smoking. It can also be used with smoked lamb or pork.*

1 pound butter or margarine
2 onions, finely chopped
5 cloves garlic, minced
1½ cups beer, such as Shiner Bock
4 lemons, quartered
½ teaspoon ground cayenne chile

2 tablespoons commercial chili
   powder
1 bunch parsley tops, minced
2 cups vegetable oil
¼ cup Worcestershire sauce
2 bay leaves

In a pot over medium heat, melt the butter, add the onions and garlic, and sauté for 4 to 5 minutes, until soft. Add the beer, squeeze in the lemon juice, and add the lemon rinds. When the foam subsides, add the remaining ingredients, turn up the heat to high, and bring to a boil. Reduce to a medium-low heat and simmer for 20 minutes.

 # Thai Lemongrass Marinade

MAKES: ½ cup
HEAT SCALE: Hot

Lemongrass makes a nice houseplant and gives you a continuous supply of lemony stalks. To start your own plant, just root a stalk in water, then plant it in a pot. Put it in partial sun, and it will grow and divide. Warning: The marinade tastes so good you will want to drink it. Go ahead and call it lemongrass tea. Use this marinade for poultry, fish, or pork, or as a dressing for a salad. Dave serves it over noodles and calls it a pseudo-curry.

1 stalk lemongrass
½ cup coconut milk
8 Thai chiles (*prik kee nu*) or
    4 serrano chiles, stemmed and
    chopped
2½ tablespoons freshly squeezed
    lime juice

3 tablespoons brown sugar
1 shallot, sliced
1 tablespoon fish sauce
1 tablespoon soy sauce
1 tablespoon chopped fresh cilantro
1 teaspoon peeled and grated fresh
    ginger

Cut off and discard the green top of the lemongrass, leaving about a 6-inch stalk. Remove any tough outer leaves. Cut the stalk into 1-inch pieces and lightly pound the stalks with the knife handle to release the flavor.

Combine the lemongrass and the coconut milk in a saucepan and simmer for 10 to 15 minutes over medium heat. Do not let it boil. Remove from the heat and strain. Discard the lemongrass.

Place all the ingredients, including the milk-lemongrass mixture, in a blender or food processor and purée until smooth.

Your Basic Beer Sop or Mop

MAKES: 4 cups
HEAT SCALE: Medium

This is an all-purpose sop that can be used with any meat or poultry. Its purpose is to keep the meat moist during the smoking process and to give the cook something to do during the long, boring smoking process. Use a small sop mop to coat the meat.

1 cup vegetable oil
4 bottles good Mexican beer, such as
    Dos Equis (2 for the recipe and 2
    for drinking)
Juice of 2 lemons
1 large onion, chopped
1 clove garlic, minced

2 tablespoons vinegar
1 teaspoon salt
1 teaspoon freshly ground black
    pepper
3 tablespoons commercial hot sauce
    of choice

In a large saucepan, combine all of the ingredients except for two of the bottles of beer. Bring to a boil over high heat, then decrease the heat to medium, and simmer for 20 minutes. Use the sop to baste any meat, but especially beef, and drink the reserved bottles of beer while you sop.

 # Texas Chilipiquín Barbecue Sauce

MAKES: 2½ cups
HEAT SCALE: Hot

The wild chiles called chiltepíns *in Mexico and the Southwest are known as chili-piquíns in Texas. We always have some of these berry-like pods available because we grow them as perennials, but they're difficult to find in markets. You may substitute any piquín or small, extremely hot chile. This is a finishing sauce for grilled or smoked beef, chicken, or pork, to be applied before serving or served on the side.*

1 onion, chopped
2 tablespoons margarine or vegetable oil
3 cloves garlic, minced
2 cups ketchup
½ cup cider vinegar
⅓ cup firmly packed brown sugar
2 teaspoons Worcestershire sauce

2 tablespoons freshly squeezed lemon juice
3 teaspoons crushed chilipiquíns or other small, hot dried chiles
2 teaspoons dry mustard
¼ teaspoon freshly ground black pepper
Salt to taste

In a small skillet over medium heat, melt the margarine, and sauté the onion until soft. Add the garlic and sauté for an additional 2 minutes.

Combine all the remaining ingredients in a separate saucepan, add the onion mixture, and whisk to blend. Bring to a boil over high heat, decrease the heat to medium and simmer uncovered for 30 minutes, stirring occasionally.

Chipotle BBQ Sauce

MAKES: approximately 4 cups
HEAT SCALE: Medium

The smoked red jalapeño, known as the chipotle chile, has become so popular that there's even a couple of cookbooks devoted to it! It works particularly well with barbecuing and grilling, both of which are associated with considerable amounts of smoke.

3 dried chipotle chiles
1½ tablespoons vegetable oil
1 onion, finely chopped
2 cloves garlic, minced
2 red bell peppers, quartered,
    stemmed, and seeded

2 onions, thickly sliced
3 tomatoes, halved
2 cups ketchup
¼ cup Worcestershire sauce
¼ cup red wine vinegar
¼ cup firmly packed brown sugar

Place the chipotle chiles in a bowl with very hot water and soak for 20 minutes to soften. Drain the chiles and chop finely. Set aside.

In a medium-sized saucepan over medium heat, heat the oil and sauté the chopped onion until soft, about 5 minutes. Add the garlic and continue to sauté for an additional 2 minutes.

Roast the peppers, thickly sliced onions, and tomatoes by grilling them over a medium fire until they are soft and slightly blackened. Remove from the heat, peel the tomatoes, then chop the vegetables.

In a large saucepan over medium high heat, combine all the ingredients and bring to a low boil. Decrease the heat to medium and simmer for 20 minutes. Remove from the heat and allow the mixture to cool, then purée in a blender or food processor until smooth. You may thin the mixture with water if you wish.

Jalapeño-Strawberry Barbecue Sauce

MAKES: 2 cups
HEAT SCALE: Medium

Sure it sounds weird, combining strawberries and jalapeños in a barbecue sauce, but fruit and chiles have an ancient history of association with barbecued meats. Serve this over or as an accompaniment to grilled or smoked pork, brisket, ribs, or chicken. This is another one of those sweet sauces that has a strong tendency to burn if applied to meat on the grill over a hot fire, so consider it a finishing sauce.

2 cups fresh strawberries, sliced
½ cup strawberry preserves
⅓ cup ketchup
2 tablespoons balsamic vinegar
2 tablespoons freshly squeezed
lemon juice
2 large cloves garlic, minced

1 teaspoon peeled and chopped fresh
ginger
½ teaspoon grated lemon zest
2 jalapeño chiles, stemmed, seeded,
and chopped
1 green onion, minced, white and
green parts
2 tablespoons chopped fresh cilantro

Place all the ingredients, except the cilantro, in a blender and purée until smooth. Simmer over medium heat in an uncovered saucepan until thickened, about 20 minutes. Remove from the heat and allow to cool. Stir in the cilantro.

Infused Oils and Flavored Vinegars

To add intense flavors to your marinades and barbecue sauces, use oils and vinegars that have been steeped or simmered in various flavors. Herbs such as rosemary, tarragon, and oregano work particularly well with vinegar, while orange peel, chiles, garlic, and basil meld well with vegetable oils. To infuse an oil or vinegar, simply add the flavoring and let steep for hours or days until the flavor is imbedded. To hasten the process, gently simmer the flavorings in the oil or vinegar, cool, and place in a bottle. Oils will last for many weeks in the refrigerator; vinegars last indefinitely.

Louisiana Barbecue Sauce

MAKES: 3 cups
HEAT SCALE: Medium

This is our version of a recipe that originally appeared in Mary Land's Louisiana Cookery *(1954). We have spiced it up a bit—okay, more than a bit—and added a few other spices. This sauce is served with grilled seafood and chicken, but if you want to sneak it onto some steamed shrimp or crawdads, we wouldn't turn you in to the food police. It will keep in the refrigerator for a week and freezes nicely.*

1 tablespoon vegetable oil
¼ cup diced onion
1 clove garlic, minced
1 (15½-ounce) can diced tomatoes, drained
⅓ cup honey
2 tablespoons white distilled vinegar
3 bay leaves

2 tablespoons Louisiana-style hot sauce
2 teaspoons dry mustard
½ teaspoon dried thyme
1½ teaspoons freshly ground black pepper
Salt to taste

Heat the oil in a skillet over medium heat, and sauté the onion until soft. Add the garlic and sauté for an additional two minutes. Transfer the onion and garlic mixture to a saucepan, add the remaining ingredients and bring to a boil over high heat. Decrease the heat to low and simmer, uncovered, for 1 hour. Remove the bay leaves, place the mixture in a blender or food processor, and process until just blended.

Malaysian Peanut Sauce

MAKES: approximately 2½ cups
HEAT SCALE: Hot

This is a version of a famous peanut sauce called kajang, *named after the town of Kajang, about twenty miles from Kuala Lumpur. It is a finishing sauce that is spread over the cooked satays of chicken, pork, beef, or even tofu. It can also be used to finish chicken breasts or pork chops if you don't want to make satays. If you prefer, tamarind juice can be substituted for the coconut milk, or use a reduced-fat coconut milk. This sauce can also be used as a dip with fresh vegetables.*

1 tablespoon peanut oil

4 green onions, chopped, white part only

4 cloves garlic, minced

2 teaspoons peeled and minced fresh ginger

½ cup chicken broth

1½ cups crunchy or smooth peanut butter

½ cup rice wine vinegar

1 tablespoon soy sauce

1 tablespoon freshly squeezed lime juice

2½ tablespoons crushed red piquín chile

2 teaspoons dark brown sugar

¼ teaspoon ground cumin

½ cup unsweetened coconut milk

In a medium-sized saucepan over medium heat, heat the oil and sauté the onion, garlic, and ginger for 3 to 4 minutes or until soft and transparent but not browned. Add the chicken broth and bring to a boil over high heat. Decrease the heat to medium-low, and stir in the remaining ingredients. Simmer, uncovered, for 10 to 15 minutes, or until slightly thickened.

Smokin' Peachy Barbecue Sauce

MAKES: 2½ cups

HEAT SCALE: Hot

This is a finishing sauce that perks up virtually any grilled meat—or vegetable for that matter. Peaches and habanero chiles complement each other and produce a sauce with fruity heat and lots of spices. If you intend to use this as a basting sauce, wait until two or three minutes before removing the meat from the grill. If you baste for any longer, the sugar in the sauce may burn.

1 (15½-ounce) can sliced peaches, drained, liquid reserved

½ cup ketchup

¼ cup firmly packed brown sugar

3 tablespoons freshly squeezed lemon juice

⅓ cup bourbon

1 teaspoon ground ginger

1 teaspoon salt

½ teaspoon dried ground habanero chile or 1 fresh chile, stemmed, seeded, and minced

½ teaspoon soy sauce

½ teaspoon ground cinnamon

¼ teaspoon ground nutmeg

¼ teaspoon ground allspice

Purée the peaches in a blender or food processor until smooth.

In a saucepan over high heat, combine all the remaining ingredients, including the peach liquid, and stir in the peach purée. Bring to a boil over high heat and then decrease the heat, and simmer over medium-low heat, stirring occasionally for 15 minutes or until it thickens. If prepared ahead of time, refrigerate and reheat before using.

Kansas City–Style Barbecue Sauce

MAKES: 1½ cups
HEAT SCALE: Medium

Here is the way sauce is made for the famous American Royal Cook-Off in Kansas City—or at least this is our take on the subject. It is truly a finishing sauce and should not be used as a marinade or a basting sauce. Go ahead and spread it liberally over ribs just off the grill, and serve plenty on the side.

1 tablespoon vegetable oil

1 small onion, chopped

2 cloves garlic, minced

1 cup ketchup

⅓ cup molasses

¼ cup white distilled vinegar

2 tablespoons commercial chili powder

2 teaspoons dry mustard

1 teaspoon celery salt

1 teaspoon paprika

1 teaspoon ground cayenne chile

½ teaspoon freshly ground black pepper

¼ cup water, more if needed

In a saucepan over medium heat, heat the oil and sauté the onion until soft. Add the garlic and sauté for an additional 2 minutes. Add the remaining ingredients and simmer over medium low heat for ½ hour or until thickened.

North Carolina Barbecue Sauce

MAKES:	2 cups
HEAT SCALE:	Medium

This is a thin, vinegar-based sauce in the tradition of eastern North Carolina. For a rough idea of the western North Carolina sauce, add 1 cup ketchup, 1 teaspoon Worcestershire sauce, and ½ teaspoon cinnamon to this recipe. This is served over smoked pork in any form—sliced or pulled.

2 cups apple cider vinegar
¼ cup firmly packed brown sugar
1 tablespoon crushed red chile
3 teaspoons salt
1½ teaspoons ground cayenne chile

1 teaspoon freshly ground black pepper
1 teaspoon freshly ground white pepper

Combine all the ingredients in a large bowl, mix well, and let stand for a couple of hours to blend the flavors. Serve the sauce as a side to or over smoked pork.

 # South Carolina Mustard Sauce

MAKES:	1¾ cups
HEAT SCALE:	Mild

In South Carolina, mustard is a dominant ingredient rather than just an incidental spice in the barbecue flavor. But vinegar makes an appearance here as well, plus some hot sauce. As in North Carolina, the sauce is used primarily over smoked pork. You could also serve this over grilled pork chops.

¾ cup yellow prepared mustard
¾ cup cider vinegar
½ cup sugar
1½ tablespoons margarine
2 teaspoons salt

2 teaspoons Worcestershire sauce
2 teaspoons Louisana-style hot sauce, or more to taste
1¼ teaspoons freshly ground black pepper

Combine all the ingredients in a saucepan over low heat, stirring until blended. Simmer over medium low heat for 30 minutes. Let stand at room temperature for 1 hour before using.

Memphis-Style Finishing Sauce

MAKES: 2½ cups
HEAT SCALE: Mild

This is the sauce that is traditionally served over smoked ribs in Memphis and other parts of Tennessee. Some cooks add prepared yellow mustard to the recipe. It can be converted into a basting sauce by adding more beer and a little more vinegar. Add more hot sauce to taste, or substitute red chile or cayenne powder.

1 cup tomato sauce
1 cup red wine vinegar
½ cup light beer
1 tablespoon butter
½ teaspoon salt

2 teaspoons Louisiana-style hot sauce
½ teaspoon freshly ground black pepper

Combine all the ingredients in a saucepan over high heat and bring to a boil, stirring constantly. Decrease the heat to medium and simmer, uncovered, for 15 minutes. Remove from the heat. Serve warm over smoked meats.

The Ancient Art of Grilling

Grilling is the oldest, most widespread and most forgiving method of cooking. Over the centuries, there have been countless refinements to the process of cooking food over fire: from grills and grates to rotisseries and turnspits to gas grills and infrared burners. These improvements have enabled us to cook an even wider repertory of ingredients on the grill, but the basic principles remain the same, as does the primal pleasure of fire-cooked food.

—Steven Raichlen, *The Barbecue Bible*

Smoked Fruit Salsa

MAKES: 2½ to 3 cups
HEAT SCALE: Medium

This thick sauce is served as an accompaniment to grilled pork, fish, or chicken. It is based on the grilled pineapples that are prepared in the taquerias *(taco stands) in Mexico. Use your favorite fruitwood chips to add a nice smoky flavor to the salsa.*

1 fresh pineapple, cut into wedges
2 large oranges, cut into wedges
1 red onion, halved widthwise
2 tablespoons plus 1 teaspoon
   vegetable oil
4 teaspoons ground chile de árbol or
   other red chile powder

2 tablespoons freshly squeezed
   orange juice
1 tablespoon freshly squeezed lime
   juice
2 teaspoons balsamic vinegar
Chopped fresh cilantro, for garnish

Brush the fruits and the onion with the 2 tablespoons oil and liberally sprinkle with 2 teaspoons chile de árbol. Start a fire in the grill—a small charcoal fire or the gas grill on low. Smoke the fruits and vegetables for 5 to 10 minutes or until they just start to soften. Remove and dice, and place in a bowl.

Whisk together the orange juice, lime juice, vinegar, 1 teaspoon vegetable oil, and the remaining 2 teaspoons of the chile de árbol. Toss with the fruit, garnish with the cilantro, and serve.

Our Favorite BBQ Cook-Off Contest Names

Texas Dead Cow Cookin' & Bean Fixin' Extravaganza,
Wichita Falls, Texas

Big Pig Jig, *Vienna, Georgia*

Swine Days, *Natchez, Mississippi*

Hogtoberfest, *Roanoke Rapids, North Carolina*

Hog Wild, *Jackson, Mississippi*

Apricot-Chile Glaze

MAKES: 1¼ cups
HEAT SCALE: Medium

A glaze is a finishing sauce that is brushed on just before the meat is removed from the grill—being careful that the sugar in the glaze does not burn. This sweet-heat recipe combines chiles, horseradish, and mustard, so it can cause rhinitis (runny nose). It is designed for chicken and duck, but it is also quite tasty with pork. Spread this glaze over smoked ham during the last hour of smoking.

⅔ cup apricot jam
⅓ cup dry white wine
¼ cup distilled or cider vinegar
3 teaspoons prepared horseradish

2 teaspoons brown sugar
1 teaspoon dry mustard
½ teaspoon ground habanero,
    cayenne, or piquín chile

Place all the ingredients in a saucepan over medium heat and simmer until the jam has melted and the ingredients are well combined. Place any leftover glaze in a container and store in the freezer.

FOUR

Fiery Appetizers
in More Ways than One

CONJURE UP in your mind all those appetizers you've been offered at parties over the years. Celery sticks with plain cream cheese. Crackers with spray cheese. Sour cream and onion soup mix dip for chips. Deviled ham salad on tiny rye bread rounds. Egg salad in rolled sandwiches. Liver sausage seasoned with ketchup. Herring in dill sauce. Folk singer Mason Williams sang about them: "Them hors doovers, ain't they sweet? / Little piece of cheese and a little piece of meat." Had enough?

Of course you have. Those appetizers have gone the way of passenger pigeon pie: They're obsolete. Why? Because they lack character: namely spice, fire, and smoke.

But we're here to help. In 1986, St. Martin's Press published our second cookbook, *Fiery Appetizers*, and the fact that it has remained in print for so many years is evidence that people want appetizers to stimulate the palate—hell, even assault it. Bland appetizers merely fill the belly, while fiery appetizers get the guests craving for more heat. At least that's the chilehead version of the way a modern menu works.

In fact, we have been known to throw parties where the food consists solely of fiery appetizers on the grill. It's our Southwestern version of a *tapas* party, and we even invite the guests to grill their own appetizers. What could be better while you're waiting for the brisket to smoke than to grill little pieces of meat that have been sitting in a hot and spicy marinade? It's also a way of putting the guests to work. Hey, smoking is hard work and you need a rest from all that frantic activity.

The appetizers in this chapter are our spicy favorites from a couple of decades of testing, partying, and chowing down. Some of them, of course, can be served as entrées, but mostly they're designed to get the guests thinking about chiles and the spicy entrées and sides yet to come.

 # Samurai Beef Sticks with Cayenne-Soy Dipping Sauce

SERVES: 4 to 6
HEAT SCALE: Medium

Here's our version of a Japanese-style appetizer that's marinated twice—once before grilling and once after. In both cases, chile is added to give a sharp accent to the sweetness of the soy sauce and brown sugar. Use low-sodium soy sauce to avoid high saltiness. We serve this as an appetizer, but the sticks can be served as an entrée with rice or used as a topping over mixed greens or the Bun Cha Salad (p. 76), a pan-Asian beef salad.

Marinade
1 tablespoon sesame seeds
⅓ cup reduced sodium soy sauce
¼ cup dry sherry or rice wine (*mirin*)
3 tablespoons brown sugar
4 cloves garlic, minced
2 tablespoons chopped green onion, white and green parts
1 teaspoon sesame oil
1 tablespoon peeled and grated fresh ginger
1 teaspoon dry mustard
2 teaspoons crushed piquín chile or other small, hot chiles
¼ teaspoon freshly ground black pepper

1½ pounds flank steak, sliced ¼ inch thick and 1 to 1½ inches wide

Cayenne-Soy Dipping Sauce
¼ cup reduced sodium soy sauce
2 tablespoons peeled and grated fresh ginger
1 teaspoon ground cayenne chile
1 tablespoon thinly sliced green onion, white and green parts
Chopped green onion, white and green parts, for garnish

To make the marinade, toast the sesame seeds in a dry skillet over medium-low heat until they start to brown. Combine the seeds with all the other ingredients for the marinade in a nonreactive bowl, add the beef, and toss well. Cover and marinate for 2 hours in the refrigerator.

Remove the beef from the marinade, reserve the liquid, and thread the beef on skewers. Transfer the reserved marinade to a saucepan and simmer over medium heat for 20 minutes. Quickly grill the beef over a hot fire, basting once with the marinade, until done, about 2 minutes per side.

To make the dipping sauce, mix all the ingredients, divide the sauce into small bowls, and garnish with the green onion. Serve the beef sticks with the dipping sauce on the side.

Skewered Spiced Peruvian Beef (Anticuchos)

SERVES: 4 to 6
HEAT SCALE: Medium

These are the famous Peruvian appetizers, sold by street vendors, and grilled to order. The customers eat the beef right off the stick. Traditionally they are made with beef hearts, but we like to use more tender and flavorful cuts of beef. With this highly acidic marinade, you can use tougher cuts if you marinate them longer. The chiles of choice here would be the native aji *chiles, but virtually any small, hot fresh chiles can be used.*

Ají Chile Marinade
2 tablespoons olive oil
1 teaspoon cumin seeds
½ cup red wine
¼ cup red wine vinegar
3 red *ají limon* chiles or red serrano
    or jalapeño chiles, stemmed,
    seeded, and chopped
2 teaspoons minced garlic
1 teaspoon soy sauce

1 teaspoon dried Mexican oregano
1 teaspoon ground achiote (annato)
    or achiote paste
1 teaspoon salt
Freshly ground black pepper

1½ pounds beef sirloin, cut into
    ¾-inch cubes

4 to 6 corn tortillas (optional)

To make the marinade, heat the oil in a small skillet over medium-low heat, and then sauté the cumin seeds for 5 minutes. Strain the oil and discard the seeds. Combine the oil and all the remaining marinade ingredients in a blender or food processor and purée until smooth.

Toss the meat in the marinade, place in a nonreactive bowl, cover, and marinate in the refrigerator for at least 2 hours—longer for tougher cuts of meat.

Thread the meat on skewers, cover, and let sit at room temperature for 20 minutes. Return the marinade to a saucepan and simmer over low heat for 20 minutes. Grill the beef over a medium-hot fire, basting frequently with the marinade for about 4 minutes on each side, until the beef is done. Cut a piece to check for doneness.

Serve these on the skewers as kebabs or as a snack sandwich wrapped in warmed corn tortillas.

Curry Satay

SERVES: 4 to 6 (24 Skewers)
HEAT SCALE: Medium

Satays, also known as sates, *are small pork brochettes or kebabs, traditionally grilled over charcoal on bamboo skewers in Southeast Asia, Indonesia, and Malaysia. This recipe also works well with chicken. You can use commercial curry powder or make your own. Red curry paste is available in Asian markets. For a tasty variation, thread fruits such as banana or pineapple chunks in between the pork cubes. Serve with any of the Asian sauces in chapter 3, such as the Thai Lemongrass Marinade (p. 33) or the Malaysian Peanut Sauce (p. 38), with a commercial chutney, or even with the Coconut-Mint Chutney (p. 146).*

Marinade
½ cup coconut milk
¼ cup white wine vinegar
2 tablespoons red curry paste
2 tablespoons curry powder
1 tablespoon sugar

1½ teaspoons ground cayenne chile
   or Thai chile (*prik kee nu*)

———————

2 pounds boneless pork, cut into
   ¾-inch cubes

To make the marinade, combine all the ingredients in a bowl. Add the pork, toss well, cover, and marinate for 2 to 3 hours in the refrigerator.

Remove the pork from the marinade. Simmer the marinade in a saucepan over medium heat for 20 minutes. Thread the pork on the skewers, putting about 6 chunks on each. Leave a 2- or 3-inch "handle" at one end, and pack the meat closely together. Grill the skewers for about 10 minutes over a medium-hot heat, basting frequently with the marinade, until browned and crisp. Cut open a sample to check for doneness.

Place the satays on a platter and serve immediately.

 ## Spice Islands Coconut-Chile Pork Kebabs with Sambal Marinade *(pictured in photo section)*

SERVES: 4
HEAT SCALE: Mild

This recipe calls for fish sauce, which is an acquired taste, so add more or less depending on how much you like it. Sambal oelek is a condiment commonly used in Indonesia and Malaysia. Sambal means hot sauce in English; it's a staple in an Indonesian kitchen and is available in Asian markets. Generally it is very spicy. It can

Holy Pork!

In earlier days, the names of pioneering restaurateurs were spoken in reverent tones, usually by the males of the family, and the infrequent meal at one of those hallowed establishments was something like worshiping in church, as eyes closed and heads shook slowly and wordlessly back and forth over the evidence of grace bestowed in the form of peppery, chopped pork. In the intervals between such rites, frequent reminiscing no doubt elevated the quality of the barbecue to mythical proportions.

—Bob Garner, *North Carolina Barbecue: Flavored by Time*

be used as a garnish or accompaniment. Here it is used as an ingredient in the mari-
nade. These kebabs are a great start to any Asian or Indian meal. Serve with your
choice of dipping sauces.

Sambal Marinade
½ cup coconut milk
2 green onions, minced, white and
    green parts
2 tablespoons commercial *sambal*
    oelek
1 tablespoon freshly squeezed lime
    juice
1 tablespoon sugar
1 tablespoon chopped fresh cilantro
2 teaspoons fish sauce

1½ pounds boneless pork, cut into
    ¾-inch cubes

Dipping Sauces
Commerical *sambal oelek,* Malaysian
    Peanut Sauce (p. 38), Vietnamese
    Pork Sauce (p. 76), or Coconut-
    Mint Chutney (p. 147)

To make the marinade, combine all the ingredients in a bowl. Add the
pork, toss well, cover, and marinate for 2 to 3 hours in the refrigerator.

Remove the pork cubes from the marinade, thread on skewers, and grill
over a medium-hot grill for about 10 minutes, until done. Cut open a
sample to check for doneness. They should be browned and crisp.

Arrange the kebabs on a serving platter and serve with the desired dipping sauce.

Just Give Us a Time Machine
and We'll Be There

Sarah Hicks Williams moved with her new husband from New York to
Clifton Grove, North Carolina, in 1852. In letters to her parents about
the differences between the North and the South, she wrote about her
husband's family: "They live more heartily. There must always be two
or three kinds of meats on Mrs. Williams' table for breakfast and dinner. Red pepper is much used to flavor meat with the famous 'barbecue' of the South, and the dish which I believe they esteem above all
others is roasted pig dressed with red pepper and vinegar."

❦ Pili Pili Pork Kebabs

SERVES: 4 to 6
HEAT SCALE: Medium

Pili pili, piri piri, *and* peri peri *are all variations on the Swahili word that simply means "pepper-pepper." It is the name of various chiles and chile-infused dishes throughout Africa. This is a fairly common dish that is traditionally cooked over hot coals.*

Peanut-Cayenne Marinade

¾ cup creamy peanut butter
⅓ cup soy sauce
3 tablespoons freshly squeezed lime
    juice
¼ cup vegetable oil
1½ tablespoons ground coriander
1 tablespoon ground cayenne chile
1 tablespoon ground cumin

1½ pounds boneless pork, cut into
    ¾-inch cubes

1½ cups chopped or ground peanuts
Chopped fresh parsley, for garnish

To make the marinade, combine all the ingredients in a bowl. Add the pork, toss well, cover, and marinate for 2 hours in the refrigerator.

Remove the pork cubes from the marinade and thread on skewers, packing the meat closely together. Brush the meat with additional marinade and then roll in the peanuts.

Grill the meat over a medium fire until crisp, but not burned, about 10 minutes. Cut open a sample to check for doneness.

To serve, place the skewers on a serving platter, and garnish with parsley.

Cape Town Sosaties

SERVES: 4 to 6
HEAT SCALE: Medium

Although considered a South African dish, sosaties originated in Malaysia, where spicy grilled meat is so popular, and was then introduced by immigrants. Sosaties are to South Africans as kebabs are to Afghanis. This is a festival dish, served at outdoor cookouts and outdoor festivals called braai. *Lamb is the meat of choice, but beef, pork, and chicken can also be used.*

1 pound boneless lamb, cut into
   1-inch cubes

Marinade
2 teaspoons garlic powder
Salt and freshly ground black pepper
2 tablespoons vegetable oil
1 onion, chopped
2 cloves garlic, chopped
⅓ cup strained apricot jam
2 tablespoons distilled white vinegar
1 tablespoon brown sugar

1 tablespoon hot curry powder
1 teaspoon ground coriander
1 teaspoon peeled and grated fresh
   ginger
1½ teaspoons ground cayenne chile
¼ teaspoon ground allspice
¼ teaspoon ground cloves
⅛ teaspoon ground cumin
¼ cup water

24 dried apricots
6 strips bacon

To prepare the meat, place the lamb in a bowl and sprinkle with the garlic powder, salt, and pepper and toss.

To make the marinade, heat the oil in a skillet over medium heat, add the onion and garlic, and sauté until soft. Combine all the ingredients, except the apricots and bacon, with the onion and garlic in a saucepan, and bring to a boil over high heat. Decrease the heat to medium and simmer for 10 minutes. Remove from the heat and let cool.

Place the meat cubes in a nonreactive bowl and cover with the marinade. Marinate, covered, in the refrigerator overnight. Transfer the meat from the marinade to a plate. Transfer the marinade to a saucepan, and simmer at medium heat for 20 minutes.

Soak the apricots in hot water for 20 minutes to plump. Drain the apricots. Cut the bacon in pieces large enough to wrap around the meat cubes.

Wrap the bacon around the meat and place them on skewers, alternating with the apricots. Grill over a medium fire, brushing with the marinade, for 15 minutes, turning the skewers often. Cut open a sample to check for doneness.

Arrange the *sosaties* on a platter. Ladle the marinade into a bowl and serve it on the side.

 # Berbere Kifto *(pictured in photo section)*

SERVES: 4 to 6
HEAT SCALE: Hot

Berbere is both the Ethiopian name for chiles and an incredibly powerful paste made from chiles and numerous spices that are used in nearly all Ethiopian dishes. Tribal customs dictate that the berbere be served over warm, fresh raw meat called kifto. But there's no way we're going to recommend serving raw meat in a barbecue book, so grill the kifto! Bebere is also an excellent treatment for chicken wings on the grill.

Berbere Paste

3 teaspoons ground cayenne chile

2 tablespoons onion powder

2 teaspoons ground ginger

1 teaspoon ground cardamom

½ teaspoon salt

½ teaspoon ground fenugreek

½ teaspoon ground cinnamon

¼ teaspoon ground cumin

¼ teaspoon freshly ground black pepper

¼ teaspoon ground nutmeg

¼ teaspoon allspice

¼ teaspoon turmeric

¼ teaspoon ground cloves

1 teaspoon minced garlic

2 tablespoons chopped red onion

2 tablespoons dry red wine

3 or more tablespoons peanut or vegetable oil

The Kifto

1½ pounds lean ground beef

3 tablespoons minced red onion

1 teaspoon ground cloves

1 egg, beaten

Chopped fresh cilantro or Italian parsley, for garnish

Going Beyond Pork and Beef

Mutton is the prime BBQ meat at the Owensboro Bar-B-Q Championship held every May in that Kentucky town. The locals, descended from Dutch settlers who raised sheep, say mutton is a natural because it needs the long smoking to release its flavor, while younger lamb does not. The other meats are smoked as well at this championship, but by far barbecued mutton is most of the ton of meat served up every day of the contest.

To make the paste, combine all the ingredients, except the oil, in a blender or food processor. With the motor running, slowly add just enough of the oil to form a paste.

To make the *kifto,* combine all the ingredients with the berbere paste in a bowl and mix well. Form into small, slightly elongated balls and place on skewers.

Grill over a medium-hot fire for about 8 minutes, until cooked through. Cut open a sample to check for doneness.

To servce, arrange the *kifto* kebabs on a serving platter, and garnish with the cilantro.

 # Margarita-Grilled Shrimp and Avocado Quesadilla

MAKES: 12 to 24 wedges
HEAT SCALE: Mild

This is one of those crossover dishes that can be served whole as an entrée or cut into wedges as an appetizer. If ever there were such a thing as a "Grilled Shrimp Mexican-Style Pizza," this would be it. Feel free to substitute chicken pieces for the shrimp if you like. Would you dare serve this with a margarita? Well, why not? We do.

Margarita Marinade

¼ cup tequila
3 tablespoons Triple Sec
2 tablespoons vegetable oil
1 tablespoon chopped fresh cilantro
1 tablespoon finely chopped onion
2 serrano or jalapeño chiles,
    stemmed, seeded, and finely
    chopped
1 teaspoon ground chipotle chile

Guacamole

2 avocados, mashed or finely
    chopped
½ tomato, chopped
2 minced serrano chiles
2 tablespoons freshly squeezed lime
    juice

1 pound shrimp, peeled and deveined
6 (7-inch) flour tortillas
Vegetable oil
1½ cups shredded Monterey Jack or
    asadero cheese
Chopped fresh cilantro

To make the marinade, combine all the ingredients in a nonreactive bowl. Add the shrimp, toss, cover, and marinate for 1 hour in the refrigerator.

To make the guacamole, combine all the ingredients in a bowl and mix well. Cover and refrigerate.

To prepare the shrimp, put them in a grilling basket and place on the grill. Shake the basket often to make sure the shrimp is grilled on all sides. Grill for about 4 minutes over a medium fire, or until the shrimp just turn pink and opaque. Remove from the fire.

Brush one side of 3 tortillas with the oil. Spread some guacamole over the other side of each tortilla. Divide the shrimp among them, sprinkle with the cheese and cilantro, and press firmly together. Cover with the remaining tortillas and brush with oil.

Grill the quesadillas over medium heat either by the indirect method (away from flames) for 5 minutes, or direct method (over flames) for 3 to 4 minutes or until the tortillas start to brown and the cheese melts. Turn once—carefully.

To serve, cut the quesadillas into wedges and top with a dollop of guacamole.

Cured and Pecan-Smoked King Salmon with Hot Sauce

SERVES: 10 or more
HEAT SCALE: Varies according to sauces added

The key to preparing salmon this way is to make certain that your smoke is rather cool, about 100°. If it is warmer, decrease the smoking time. This recipe takes a fair amount of time, but you spend most of it waiting rather than working. The selection of sauces served with it is up to the cook, so feel free to experiment.

The Cure

2½ cups kosher salt
¾ cup firmly packed brown sugar
1 tablespoon freshly ground black
    pepper
1 teaspoon ground oregano
1 teaspoon crushed dill weed

2 large salmon fillets, about 2 to 5
    pounds each, or 5 small but
    thicker fillets
Crackers, such as Wheat Thins or
    water crackers
Commercial habanero hot sauce
Commercial sherry pepper hot sauce
Commercial spicy mustard
Commercial creamy horseradish
    sauce

To make the cure, combine the ingredients in a bowl and mix well. Place a sheet of plastic wrap on a baking sheet and spread about a ⅛-inch thick layer of the cure blend over it. Place the fillets on the cure and top with another ⅛ inch of cure. Cover the fillets with plastic wrap, and cure in the refrigerator for at least 2 hours; a 4-hour cure is preferable. Remove the fillets from the wrap and rinse the cure off each fillet. Allow the fillets to air-dry for about 2 hours.

Prepare a fire in the smoker's firebox with pecan wood or other fruit or nut hardwood of choice, such as apple, apricot, peach, or walnut. When the fire stabilizes and the smoke is no longer hot, place the fillets skin-side down on racks or in the aluminum baking pan.

Smoke the fillets for 4 to 5 hours, depending on their thickness. Regularly check to make sure that the fish is smoking, not rapidly cooking.

Serve the salmon over crackers of choice topped with any of the sauces. Refrigerate any leftovers: They will keep for weeks.

Bayou Shrimp with Cajun Butter

SERVES: 4 to 6
HEAT SCALE: Medium

Shrimp prepared in this manner illustrates the Louisiana love of herbs, spices, and, let's not forget, their ubiquitous hot sauce. This recipe can also be served as an entrée by serving the shrimp over white rice and topped with a few spoonfuls of Cajun Butter.

Bayou Shrimp Marinade
½ cup peanut or vegetable oil
3 tablespoons chopped green onion,
   white and green parts
2 cloves garlic, chopped
2 teaspoons freshly ground black
   pepper
1 teaspoon ground cumin
½ teaspoon ground cayenne chile
½ teaspoon dried rosemary
½ teaspoon dried thyme
¼ teaspoon dried oregano

Cajun Butter
½ cup butter
½ teaspoon basil
½ teaspoon dried marjoram
¼ teaspoon dried thyme
¼ teaspoon ground white pepper
¼ teaspoon freshly ground black
   pepper
¼ teaspoon garlic powder
2 teaspoons Louisiana-style hot
   sauce

1 pound large shrimp, peeled and
   deveined, tails left on
Chopped fresh parsley, for garnish

To make the marinade, combine all the ingredients in a bowl. Add the shrimp, toss to coat, cover, and marinate for 1 hour in the refrigerator. Transfer the shrimp to a plate. Pour the marinade into a saucepan and simmer over medium heat for 20 minutes.

To prepare the cajun butter, melt the butter in a saucepan over low heat. Stir in the remaining ingredients and remove from the heat. You might need to warm it up a little before serving. Place the shrimp in a grill basket and grill over a medium fire for 4 to 7 minutes, turning and basting frequently with the marinade.

Arrange the shrimp around a platter and garnish with the parsley. Place a bowl of cajun butter in the center for dipping and serve with toothpicks for spearing.

Grilled Crab-Stuffed Cherry Peppers

(pictured in photo section)

SERVES: 6
HEAT SCALE: Mild

We don't usually think about grilling pickled peppers, but for some reason they turn out great. Just remember not to overgrill the peppers or they may blacken on the outside. Note that although some commercial cherry peppers are called "hot" by the manufacturers, they are usually rather mild. This recipe is reminiscent of the wonderful canned stuffed jalapeños from Mexico—in fact, this recipe works with pickled jalapeños as well.

12 pickled "hot" cherry peppers
Lettuce leaves, for garnish
Chopped fresh cilantro, for garnish

Crab Filling
3 tablespoons crabmeat
   (canned is fine)

1½ tablespoons cream cheese
4 teaspoons dried bread crumbs
2 tablespoons chopped fresh cilantro
1 teaspoon milk
¼ teaspoon garlic salt

What about Texas and Kansas City?

Barbecue *is* a Southern cultural icon. Bound to the long tradition of Southern history, barbecue has become more than just pit-smoked pork. Its ties to history, culture, and food ways make it one of the few aspects of life in the South that has not been significantly homogenized by the "Americanization of Dixie." Most Northerners do not understand the concept of barbecue and are perfectly content to continue grilling hot dogs in the back yard, thank you very much. Barbecue remains a Southern phenomenon, one that can be embraced by Southerners of every race, class, and political orientation. What constitutes true barbecue is another question, but arguing over barbecue beats arguing about other, more incendiary (no pun intended) topics

—Laura Dove, "BBQ—A Southern Cultural Icon"

To prepare the peppers, cut out the stems and core them. The opening should be wide enough to fill. Try using the tip of a vegetable peeler for this chore.

To make the filling, combine all the ingredients in a bowl and mix well. Stuff the cherry peppers and place on a mesh screen.

Grill over a medium fire for 3 to 4 minutes until hot. Do not turn or the filling might fall out.

To serve, line a platter with lettuce leaves, arrange the peppers on top, and garnish with a little cilantro.

Tunisian Hot Vegetable Dip (Slata Mechouia)

MAKES: approximately 2 cups
HEAT SCALE: Medium

This recipe is based on the Tunisian grilled salads: Mechouia means roasted. It can easily be prepared on the grill and served as a relish, dip, or spread. As might be expected, it can also be served with a flat, unleavened bread such as pita. Use a mortar and pestle for a traditional method of grinding the grilled vegetables, or just mash and mix with a fork in a bowl. For a much hotter dip, substitute jalapeño chiles.

1 red or yellow bell pepper, halved, stemmed, and seeded
2 tomatoes
1 small onion, halved
4 green New Mexican chiles or poblano chiles
3 cloves garlic
2 to 3 tablespoons olive oil

2 teaspoons freshly squeezed lemon juice
1 tablespoon caraway or cumin seeds
1 tablespoon chopped brine-cured black olives
Chopped fresh parsley, for garnish
1 small loaf French bread

Place the bell pepper, tomatoes, onion, chiles, and garlic on a medium-hot grill, and grill 5 to 10 minutes, until the skins become charred and blistered. The onions will take longer to cook than the rest of the vegetables. Remove the vegetables from the grill, place in a bowl, and cover with a damp cloth to loosen the skins. Remove the skins, but don't worry—a few charred pieces will add an interesting flavor dimension. Mash the vegetables together with a fork and place the mixture in a bowl.

Mix together the remaining ingredients, except for the parsley and bread, pour over the vegetables, and gently toss. Transfer to a serving bowl.

Serve the dip in a bowl, garnished with the parsley, with the bread on the side. Encourage the guests to tear the bread into chunks and dip in the mixture.

Sundried Tomato and Olive Tapenade Bruschetta

SERVES: 6
HEAT SCALE: Medium

The Italian word bruschetta *comes from the verb* bruscare, *to roast over coals. Italian bruschetta, traditionally, are thick slices of Italian bread that are grilled and then rubbed with olive oil and garlic. This is our heated-up version: We simply couldn't resist the temptation to add chile. Day-old bread works best on the grill. Grilled focaccia wedges also make a great bruschetta.*

The topping can be made in a food processor, but be sure to pulse it so that it is chunky, not smooth.

⅓ cup sundried tomatoes, dry-packed or in oil
⅓ cup olive oil
3 tablespoons chopped walnuts
2 tablespoons grated Parmesan cheese
2 tablespoons chopped black olives
1 tablespoon capers, rinsed
1 tablespoon crushed hot red chile

1 tablespoon chopped fresh Italian parsley
1 tablespoon freshly squeezed lemon juice
Salt

6 slices day-old Italian or country-style bread, sliced ¾ inch thick

My First Barbecue Bible

Before Steven Raichlen—hell, even before James Beard—there was the original "Barbecue Bible," entitled *Sunset Barbecue Book*. It was published by Lane Publishing Company of Menlo Park, California, in 1938 and is believed to be the first book ever published on home barbecuing. The second edition was called *Sunset Barbecue Cook Book* and was published in 1950. I have, passed down from my father, Dick DeWitt, the third edition that was published in 1959. It cost $1.95 as a trade paperback. To this day I think it is one of the most informative books ever published on grilling and barbecue, and is one of the few books that shows you, step by step, how to make and use your own firepit. The chapter on smoke cooking is excellent and shows how smokers were jury-rigged long before manufactured home smokers became available. And you just don't find recipes for Spit-Roasted Calf's Liver any more!

If using dry-packed tomatoes, cover with hot water and allow to sit for 30 minutes to rehydrate, then drain. If using tomatoes in oil, place in a saucepan along with the oil from the jar rather than additional olive oil and heat for 2 to 3 minutes, then allow to steep for 30 minutes. Remove the tomatoes, chop finely, and save the oil. Combine all the ingredients for the topping and place in a serving bowl. Cover and let sit for 30 minutes to blend the flavors.

Brush the bread on both sides with the reserved oil and grill on each side for 1 to 2 minutes over a medium fire. Press down on the bread with a spatula to make grill marks on the bread.

To serve, arrange the bread on a platter and place the topping in a bowl. Guests can spoon the topping over the bread and enjoy.

FIVE

For Carnivores Only

The Meating Place of Spice and Smoke

THE FIRST OUTDOOR COOK to use chile peppers during a barbecue was Jaguar Claw, a "paleo-American" who lived in the Amazon Basin about 20,000 years ago. He had dispatched the world's largest rodent with his spear, butchered the carcass with his new flint carving knife into 1-inch chunks, and was contemplating boiling the pieces for dinner.

"Boiled water-pig is boring," said Macaw Feather, his lovely wife. "Rub the meat with this powder and then grill it on sticks over the fire."

"What is this red powder?" asked Jaguar Claw.

"Made from bird berries," answered Macaw Feather. "The birds eat them. They are hot to the taste and will flavor the meat."

Jaguar Claw followed Macaw Feather's suggestion, rubbed the meat with the red powder, and let it sit for a while. Then he skewered it on thin sticks and held it above the fire until it was cooked medium-rare.

Later, as the well-fed couple passed the intensely flavored grilled meat around to the rest of the tribe in the jungle clearing, Jaguar Claw asked: "What shall we call this food?"

"How about Chile-Rubbed Grilled Capybara Kebabs?" suggested Macaw Feather.

Well, it could have happened that way.

There is no doubt that the collision of chiles and barbecue first happened in South America, the ancestral birthplace of the wild chiles that were the precursors to the hundreds of domesticated varieties we cook with today. First picked in the wild, they became an indispensable season-

The West Texas Grilling Experience

A big, thick, char-grilled T-bone, a pile of hot mashed potatoes, and an ice-cold Lone Star beer—that's my idea of West Texas cowboy cuisine. Lots of highly trained chefs wouldn't be caught dead serving this kind of simple, old-fashioned American food in their restaurants, but I get away with it because I'm not really a chef. I'm just a cowboy in the kitchen.

—Grady Spears and Robb Walsh, *A Cowboy in the Kitchen*

ing and vegetable when the advent of agriculture changed the way humans acquired food. And once Columbus brought chile seeds back to the Old World, chiles would become a part of the outdoor cooking traditions all over the world.

The recipes that follow illustrate the use of chiles in their myriad forms when combined with meat, heat, and smoke. Don't be worried if you cannot find a particular chile—we've suggested substitutes for the more unusual varieties. Often you can make meat substitutions too, such as lamb for beef, or one type of game for another.

A note on pork: When Nancy and I were growing up, our parents, a continent apart, drilled into our heads that pork had to be cooked to well-done to avoid the roundworm known as *Trichinosis spiralis*. A lot has changed since then. Pigs are no longer fed garbage, so trichinosis has been virtually eliminated from pigs in the United States. And besides, a temperature of 140° was enough to kill the worm, so why cook the pork to 180°? The National Pork Council now recommends cooking pork to 160°, or medium but still juicy. We concur.

Grilled Green Chile–Stuffed Pepper Steaks Wrapped in Bacon

SERVES: 4
HEAT SCALE: Medium

This is one of our favorite ways of grilling steaks. We find ourselves using the basic recipe and altering it again and again. The combination of the various peppers and the chiles provides different spice and heat sensations in the mouth, and the green chile pulls all the tastes together. Serve these steaks with mashed potatoes and our Grilled Spring Asparagus with Spicy Lemon Mop (p. 167). Leftover steak can be turned into a fabulous Southwest steak sandwich by thinly slicing it and putting it on sourdough bread with Muenster cheese and more chile.

4 boneless ribeye steaks, filet
   mignon, or sirloin steaks, 1 to 2
   inches thick
4 green New Mexican chiles,
   stemmed, seeded, roasted, and
   peeled
4 strips uncooked bacon

2 tablespoons each red, white, and
   black peppercorns
2 tablespoons Caribbean habanero
   sauce
2 tablespoons Worcestershire sauce
2 tablespoons soy sauce
2 tablespoons rice wine vinegar
½ teaspoon garlic powder

Slice the steaks horizontally to create a pocket, but do not cut all the way through the steak. Place a green chile in each of the pockets. Wrap a strip of bacon around each steak horizontally and secure with a toothpick.

Place the peppercorns in a towel and pound with a hammer or mortar until coarsely crushed. Press the pepper into each side of the steak.

To make the marinade, combine the habanero sauce, Worcestershire sauce, soy sauce, vinegar, and garlic powder in a bowl. Place the steaks in a non-metallic pan, pour the marinade over the meat, and marinate in the refrigerator for 2 or 3 hours. Bring the steaks to room temperature before grilling.

Grill the steaks over a medium-hot fire for 8 to 10 minutes, turning often, for rare, and 12 to 16 minutes for medium-rare. For rare steaks, the internal temperature should be 140°, for medium-rare steaks, 150°. Feel free to slice it to check for doneness.

Place the steaks on individual plates and serve.

VARIATION: For those not enamored of peppercorns, omit and wrap the steaks in peppered bacon.

 # Chimayo Chile Steaks with Chipotle Potatoes

SERVES: 4
HEAT SCALE: Medium

From the little village of Chimayo comes what many chileheads consider to be the finest tasting red chile, and we agree. We use it in our enchilada sauces and for making rubs such as this one. The smoky taste of the chipotle potatoes is a nice complement to the grilled steak. Serve the steak and potatoes with mixed green and yellow snap beans, peas, or a vegetable of choice.

Chimayo Rub
2 tablespoons ground red Chimayo
    or New Mexico chile
1 tablespoon sugar
1 tablespoon ground cinnamon
2 teaspoons ground coriander
1 teaspoon salt
1½ teaspoons ground cumin
¼ teaspoon ground thyme

Chipotle Potatoes
2 large baking potatoes
2 to 3 tablespoons milk
1 tablespoon chipotle chiles in
    adobo, chopped
¼ teaspoon garlic powder
Chopped chives, for garnish
Salt and freshly ground black pepper

4 New York strip steaks
Olive oil, for brushing

Preheat the oven to 350°. To make the dry rub, combine all the ingredients in a bowl.

To make the potatoes, bake until just done, about 1 hour. Scoop out the flesh and whip with the milk, chipotles, and garlic powder. Add salt and pepper to taste. Use just enough milk to hold the potatoes together. Stuff the potato mixture back into the skins. Place the potatoes on the grill, away from the direct flame, and heat the grill.

When the grill is hot, brush the steaks with the olive oil and liberally coat with dry rub. Grill the steaks for 12 to 16 minutes, turning often, for rare (internal temperature: 140°); or 15 to 20 minutes for medium-rare. You can slice it open to check for doneness, too.

Remove the potatoes from the grill and garnish with the chives. Serve the steaks on individual plates accompanied by the chipotle potatoes.

 # Hoisin Beef Ribs   *(pictured in photo section)*

SERVES: 4
HEAT SCALE: Medium

This is our version of a Korean rib dish that is usually served as individual ribs. If these ribs were to be smoked, we would not boil them first. Since they tend to be fatty, however, we boil these before grilling. Serve the ribs with fried rice, stir-fried vegetables,

Vote-Buying BBQ

In the nineteenth century, barbecue was a feature at church picnics and political rallies as well as at private parties. A barbecue was a popular and relatively inexpensive way to lobby for votes, and the organizers of political rallies would provide barbecue, lemonade, and usually a bit of whiskey. These gatherings were also an easy way for different classes to mix. Barbecue was not a class-specific food, and large groups of people from every stratum could mix to eat, drink and listen to stump speeches. Journalist Jonathan Daniels, writing in the mid-twentieth century, maintained that, "Barbecue is the dish which binds together the taste of both the people of the big house and the poorest occupants of the back end of the broken-down barn."

—Laura Dove, "BBQ—A Southern Cultural Icon"

and cucumber slices sprinkled with hot ground red chile. Hoisin sauce and Asian chilli sauce are available in Asian markets.

3 pounds beef ribs

3 tablespoons hoisin sauce

3 tablespoons chopped green onion, white and green parts

2 tablespoons freshly squeezed orange juice

2 tablespoons Asian chilli sauce with ginger

2 tablespoons rice vinegar

2 tablespoons peeled and chopped fresh ginger

1 tablespoon crushed piquín chile or other small, red chiles

1 tablespoon brown sugar

1 tablespoon grated orange zest

2 cloves garlic, minced

Cut the ribs into individual pieces. Place in a pot, cover with water, and bring to a boil over high heat. Decrease the heat to medium-low and simmer, uncovered, for 30 minutes. Drain the ribs.

Combine all the remaining ingredients and let sit at room temperature while the ribs are cooking.

Grill the ribs over a medium fire for about 10 minutes without basting. Move the ribs away from direct flames and cook about 10 minutes longer, basting consistently with the sauce until crisp.

To serve, heap the ribs on a platter.

Defining a Perfectly Grilled Ground Beef Patty

The meaning of the burger is as a kind of common denominator of the beef experience, with all the flavor, aroma, tenderness, and juiciness in a cheap and accessible form. The meatiness, the beefiness, the succulence of the fat are all there in that unassuming little patty. For perhaps for the first time ever, the hunger for all that beef is, for all that beef represents, can easily be satisfied, is available to almost everyone—and it is perfectly clear that almost everyone wants it. It provides a genuine fulfillment of that atavistic craving in all of us for tender roasted meat running with fat and juice, a hunger that seems to have been a common part of our shared experiences as human beings.

—Elisabeth Rozin, *The Primal Cheeseburger*

Chipotle Barbecued Ribs with Chile-Grilled Potato Wedges

SERVES: 4
HEAT SCALE: Hot

There's something magical about chipotle chiles and grilling—maybe it's the fact that these chiles were created with smoke. Serve with spicy black bean and corn salad and buttermilk biscuits. And pick a dessert from chapter 10 to finish off the meal.

Chipotle Barbecue Sauce

4 dried chipotle chiles, stemmed
3 dried red New Mexican chiles, stemmed and seeded
2 teaspoons vegetable oil
1 onion, chopped
4 cloves garlic, chopped
1 (12-ounce) can beer
3 cups ketchup
½ cup strongly brewed coffee
1½ tablespoons cider vinegar
¼ cup molasses
3 tablespoons Dijon mustard
2 teaspoons Worcestershire sauce
½ teaspoon freshly ground black pepper

Chile-Grilled Potato Wedges

2 cloves garlic, minced
1 teaspoon ground red New Mexican chile
2 tablespoons olive oil
2 potatoes, unpeeled, cut into wedges
2 green onions, finely chopped, white and green parts

Salt and freshly ground black pepper
4 pounds pork ribs

To make the sauce, cover the dried chiles with hot water and let sit for 30 minutes to soften. Drain the chiles and discard the water. Heat the oil in a saucepan over medium heat, add the onion, and sauté until softened. Add the garlic and sauté for an additional 2 minutes. Add the remaining sauce ingredients, including the chiles, and bring the mixture to a boil over high heat. Decrease the heat to medium and simmer for 20 minutes. Remove from the heat, place in a blender or food processor, and purée until smooth. Strain if desired.

Tips from the Expert

Rib doctor Guy Simpson says that backyard barbecuers often don't have the opportunity to learn the tricks of the trade that competitive barbecuers use all of the time. He says you'll be on your way to mouthwatering ribs if you give the following technique a try:

🌿 To skin baby back ribs, turn the ribs over and find the second bone in. Take a Phillips head screwdriver and put a hole in the rib big enough to put your finger through. Put your finger through the hole and pull off the membrane on the back of the ribs. This will allow the ribs to get smoke from both sides.

🌿 Barbecuing can be a lot of trouble for just one dinner. Simpson suggests rolling the rack of ribs up into a tube shape and fastening them with string. By doing this, and standing them on end in the smoker, you can prepare many ribs at one time. Simpson says the smoked ribs freeze beautifully for later use—but cut them apart first.

To make the potatoes, combine the garlic, chile, and olive oil and set aside in order to blend the flavors.

Liberally salt and pepper the ribs. Grill over a medium-hot grill for 10 minutes. Move the ribs away from the direct flame and continue to grill for 1 hour. Brush with the sauce during the last 10 minutes of grilling.

While the ribs are cooking, toss the potatoes in the seasoned oil until well coated. Place in a grill basket and grill for 15 minutes over direct flame until browned, shaking the basket often.

To serve, cut the ribs apart and pile on a platter. Serve with additional sauce on the side. Toss the potatoes with the green onions and place in a serving bowl.

Argentinian Steak Parrilla with Chimichurri Sauce

SERVES: 4 to 6
HEAT SCALE: Medium

A parrilla is a simple grill in Argentina, but oh what wonders it can create! As barbecue expert Steven Raichlen noted, "Argentina can be a forbidding place for a vegetarian." Chimichurri is the sauce most commonly served with beef straight from the parrilla, and there are dozens—if not hundreds—of variations of it, as well as debate about whether it should contain chiles. You know which side we favor, and our version of chimichurri *contains green* ají amarillo.

Steak Rub
2 tablespoons ground red *ají* chile or red New Mexican chile
1 teaspoon dried oregano
1 teaspoon sugar
¼ teaspoon ground cumin
½ teaspoon salt

3 pounds sirloin steak, 2 inches thick

Chimichurri Sauce
¼ cup red wine vinegar
4 cloves garlic, chopped

3 green *ají amarillo* or jalapeño chiles, stemmed, seeded, and chopped
1 bay leaf, stemmed
1 small onion, finely chopped
¾ cup chopped fresh parsley
¼ cup chopped fresh oregano, or 2 tablespoons dried oregano
½ teaspoon salt
1 teaspoon freshly ground black pepper
¼ cup olive oil

To make the steak rub, combine all the ingredients in a bowl. Rub well into the steak, place in a large sealable plastic bag, and marinate in the refrigerator for 2 to 3 hours, or preferably overnight.

To make the sauce, combine the vinegar, garlic, *ají amarillo* chiles, and bay leaf in a food processor or blender and process until smooth. Add the onion, parsley, oregano, salt, and pepper and pulse until blended but not puréed. Whisk in the oil and allow to sit for a couple of hours to blend the flavors.

Before grilling, remove the meat from the refrigerator and bring to room temperature.

Grill the steak over a medium-hot fire for about 20 minutes, turning often for medium-rare (150° internal temperature). Remove the steak from the grill and let it sit for 5 minutes.

To serve, slice the meat against the grain and arrange on a serving platter. Ladle some of the chimichurri sauce over the meat and serve the remainder on the side.

 ## Brazilian Mixed Grill: Churrasco with Molho Campanha

SERVES: 6 to 8
HEAT SCALE: Medium

Restaurants in Brazil called churrascarias *sell spit-roasted meats to order, and the skewers the meat is grilled on are actually swords. A* churrasco *is basically a Brazilian mixed barbecue, featuring beef and pork, but feel free to throw in a few sausages, as that's the way it's done in Brazil. Molho Campanha is the Brazilian version of the Mexican* pico de gallo *salsa. It's best to prepare it fresh, as it doesn't keep well. This is a lot of food, great for a small party; if you're serving a smaller group, just grill one of the meats. The* malagueta *chile used in the first basting sauce is a relative of the tabasco chile and is a favorite in Brazil. As for the chile in the pork basting sauce, many*

High on the Hog

The English language first took note of barbecue in 1661; and in 1732, Alexander Pope implored: "Send me, Gods! A whole Hog barbecu'd." Once conjoined, the two words have since been difficult to part. As an adjective, barbecue can be applied to anything on the grill; as a noun, it means one thing and one thing alone. In the South especially, but everywhere else too, save the deepest sheep or cattle country, the fortune of barbecue has always been tied to the fortune of the pig.

—John Thorne, "Serious Pig"

habanero relatives grow in the Amazon Basin, where the species was domesticated. Note that this recipe requires advance preparation. Serve this with achiote-spiced rice, sautéed greens and onions, and a tropical fruit salad.

Habanero Basting Sauce
½ cup sugar
2 tablespoons salt
1 cup water
6 juniper berries, bruised (lightly bashed all over with a spoon)
2 habanero chiles, stemmed, seeded, and chopped
1 teaspoon freshly ground white peppercorns
1 teaspoon freshly ground black pepper
1 teaspoon freshly ground coriander seeds
3 bay leaves, crushed
4 whole cloves
1 teaspoon dried thyme

4 boneless loin pork chops

Malagueta Basting Sauce
½ cup white distilled vinegar
½ cup freshly squeezed lime juice
½ cup red wine
6 fresh malagueta, tabasco, or serrano chiles
1 small onion, finely chopped
2 cloves garlic, minced
1 tablespoon sugar
1 tablespoon chopped fresh oregano, or 1 teaspoon dried oregano
1 teaspoon dried thyme
1 teaspoon salt
Freshly ground black pepper

2 pounds T-bone steak, 1-inch thick

Molho Campanha Salsa
2 tomatoes, coarsely chopped
1 large onion, finely chopped
1 small bell pepper, stemmed, seeded, and coarsely chopped
½ cup red wine vinegar
3 or 4 dried malagueta peppers or piquín chiles, crushed
1 teaspoon chopped fresh cilantro

To make the basting sauce and pork chops, place the pork in a nonreactive bowl. Combine the sugar, salt, and water in a bowl and stir until dissolved. Add the remaining ingredients and mix well. Pour the marinade over the pork and add water to cover the pork, if necessary. Cover and marinate in the refrigerator overnight.

To make the basting sauce and steak, place all the ingredients for the sauce in a blender or food processor and purée. Transfer to a nonreactive bowl and allow to sit for a couple of hours to blend the flavors. Marinate the steak in the mixture for 1 to 2 hours.

To make the salsa, combine all the ingredients and place in a serving bowl.

Bring both the meats to room temperature. To prepare the beef, drain the meat and transfer the marinade to a pot. Bring the marinade to a boil over high heat then decrease the heat to medium, and simmer for 20 minutes. To prepare the pork, remove from the marinade and place on a plate. Discard the pork marinade.

Grill the beef over a medium-hot fire, basting frequently with the marinade, and turning often, for 10 to 12 minutes for medium rare.

Grill the pork for 10 to 12 minutes, turning occasionally, until done to 160°.

Remove the meat from the grill and allow to sit for 5 minutes. To serve, slice the steaks against the grain in thin strips and place on a large serving platter. Arrange the pork on the platter. Pass around along with the salsa.

Just Give Us a Time Machine and We'll Be There, Part 2

Way back when the Dons first came to California, grilled meat was a part of every festive gathering. A huge fire was made, a freshly killed beef hung in the shade of a tree, the vaqueros and their ladies cut off pieces every time that hunger called, and cooked it over the waiting fire. It wasn't only charcoal grilling that was practiced by those Californians of the past, they also had their huge pit barbecues even as today."

—Helen Evans Brown, quoted by Evan Jones in *American Food*

Carnitas-Filled Tortillas with Chile de Árbol and Tomatillo Salsa

SERVES: 4
HEAT SCALE: Medium

Carnitas *is the Spanish diminutive for* carne *and means little pieces of meat, usually pork, that are cooked in many different ways throughout Mexico. Fried and topped with chile sauce,* carnitas *make a great breakfast side dish, or grilled, as in this recipe, they can be a delicious entrée when wrapped in a warmed corn tortilla with a grilled onion and salsa. We prefer the large Mexican bulb onion, a type of spring onion, but if you can't find any, use large green onions with the green tops left on.*

This recipe makes great hands-on luncheon soft tacos or burritos if you use flour tortillas. Serve with seasoned pinto beans or our Frijoles Borrachos (p. 109)

Chipotle-Ancho Chile Paste
⅓ cup vegetable oil
3 tablespoons freshly squeezed lime
    juice
3 tablespoons ground ancho chile
1 tablespoon ground chipotle chile
2 tablespoons chopped fresh cilantro
1 tablespoon garlic powder
1 tablespoon ground cumin
1½ teaspoons salt
1 teaspoon freshly ground black
    pepper

1½ pounds boneless pork, trimmed
    and cut into 1-inch cubes

Chile de Árbol and Tomatillo Salsa
6 to 8 dried chiles de árbol, stemmed
1 tablespoon vegetable oil
4 cloves garlic
2 tablespoons chopped onion
1 (8-ounce) can tomatillos, drained
1 tablespoon distilled white vinegar

1 bunch large green onions, white
    and green parts
2 tablespoons vegetable oil
2 teaspoons ground ancho chile
8 corn tortillas

To prepare the chile paste, combine all the ingredients in a bowl and mix well. Rub the pork cubes with the paste until well covered. Marinate in a nonreactive bowl, covered, in the refrigerator for 2 hours.

To make the salsa, rinse the chiles and slit them open lengthwise. In a sauté pan, heat the oil over medium heat and sauté the chiles until lightly browned. Add the garlic and onion and continue to sauté until the onions are lightly browned. Place the tomatillos, the vinegar, and the onion-garlic mixture in a blender or food processor and purée, adding a little water if necessary for a smooth consistency.

Remove the pork cubes from the refrigerator. Thread the pork cubes on skewers. Brush the onions with oil and sprinkle with the ground chile. Grill the pork over a medium fire for 10 to 15 minutes, until well-done and crisp. Cut open a cube to test for doneness. Place the onions on the grill and cook for about 4 minutes turning often, until they are browned but not burned. Meanwhile, warm the tortillas in aluminum foil on the grill, away from direct flames.

Remove everything from the grill and the *carnitas* from the skewers. Place the *carnitas* in the tortillas, top with onions, and cover with some of the salsa. Wrap up the tortilla and serve, or serve separately and have the guests assemble their own.

 # Thai Ginger Pork Steaks

SERVES: 4
HEAT SCALE: Medium

Pork is a preferred meat in China and Southeast Asia, so it is not surprising to find it combined with chiles and traditional Asian seasonings. This marinade is also excellent with chicken and fish. Serve the grilled pork steaks with white rice and a crisp salad such as the Asian Chile Slaw (p. 139).

Thai Ginger Marinade

2 tablespoons rice wine vinegar or
  dry sherry
2 tablespoons tomato sauce
2 tablespoons soy sauce
1 tablespoon brown sugar
2 tablespoons peeled and minced
  fresh ginger
1 tablespoon peanut or vegetable oil

6 small Thai (*prik kee nu*) chiles or
  3 serrano or jalapeño chiles,
  stemmed and minced
1 clove garlic, minced
1 teaspoon Asian fish sauce

4 pork steaks
2 cups cooked white rice

To make the marinade, place all the ingredients in a blender or food processor and purée until smooth. Transfer to a bowl and let sit for an hour to blend the flavors. Cover the pork steaks completely with the marinade and let sit in a glass bowl for 3 hours, covered, in the refrigerator.

Remove the steaks from the refrigerator and bring them to room temperature. Grill the pork over a medium fire for 10 to 15 minutes, turning often and basting frequently with the marinade until the internal temperature reaches 160°, or cut open to test for doneness if you prefer.

To serve, place the steaks on individual plates with a scoop of rice.

VARIATION: You can use any leftover marinade as a serving sauce, but be sure to first simmer it in a saucepan over medium heat for 20 minutes.

 # Vietnamese Chile and Garlic–Grilled Pork with Bun Cha Salad

SERVES: 4
HEAT SCALE: Medium

This North Vietnamese specialty is traditionally prepared on small charcoal grills that don't require much fuel. Bun cha is rice vermicelli, thin brittle white rice noodles that are used in soups and salads and, as in this recipe, are served cold as an accompaniment to grilled dishes. The bun cha noodles are best if made an hour or two ahead, covered, and kept in the refrigerator or at room temperature. This recipe can also be prepared with beef.

Vietnamese Pork Sauce
¼ cup freshly squeezed lime juice
3 tablespoons fish sauce (*nam pla*)
3 tablespoons sugar
2 teaspoons peanut oil

2 cloves garlic, minced
3 green Thai (*prik kee nu*) or jalapeño
    chiles, stemmed and sliced thinly
    into rounds
¼ cup water

Chile and Garlic–Grilled Pork

2 tablespoons fish sauce (*nam pla*)
1 tablespoon freshly squeezed lime
  juice
1 tablespoon Asian chilli garlic sauce
2 shallots, finely chopped
¾ teaspoon sugar
Freshly ground black pepper
1 (1-pound) boneless pork butt,
  trimmed of fat and thinly sliced,
  then cut into 1 by 2-inch pieces

Bun Cha Salad

¼ pound dried rice vermicelli
2 cups shredded lettuce or spinach
¼ cup peeled and diced cucumber
¼ cup shredded carrot
¼ cup coarsely chopped fresh
  cilantro
¼ cup chopped fresh mint
¼ cup toasted unsalted peanuts

To make the accent sauce, combine all the ingredients in a bowl and mix until the sugar dissolves. Allow to sit, covered, for 1 to 2 hours to blend the flavors.

To make the pork, combine in a bowl the fish sauce, lime juice, chilli garlic sauce, shallots, sugar, and black pepper and mix well. Add the pork and marinate for an hour in the refrigerator.

To make the salad, in a large bowl soak the noodles in warm water for 20 minutes, then drain. Bring a large pot of water to a boil and add the noodles. Using chopsticks or a wooden spoon, gently lift and separate the noodles to prevent them from clumping. Cook no more than 3 minutes. They should be al dente. Drain the noodles and rinse well with cold water.

Grill the pork slices over a medium-hot fire for 1 to 2 minutes per side, turning often, until the meat is slightly charred. Remove the pork from the grill and place on a plate.

To serve, divide the noodles among 4 shallow bowls or plates and arrange the lettuce, cucumber, and carrot over the noodles. Top the salad with the pork slices, and spoon some of the accent sauce over the meat. Serve the remaining sauce, cilantro, mint, and peanuts in separate bowls for sprinkling over the top as a garnish for the salad.

Barbecued Pork Adobo Sandwiches with Puerto Rican Mojo Sauce

SERVES: 4 to 6
HEAT SCALE: Hot

Because of the extent of Spain's influence throughout the world, adobos show up all the way from the Philippines to Puerto Rico. There are almost an infinite number of variations, but most have a vinegar base. Be sure to inject the marinade or cut slits in the pork so that the marinade penetrates the meat. Serve with Habanero-Spiced Black Beans (p. 81), and avocado and grapefruit slices. Mojo is an oil- and citrus-based hot sauce used primarily with pork.

The Adobo

1½ cups freshly squeezed orange
    juice
⅓ cup cider vinegar
¼ cup freshly squeezed lime juice
¼ cup dry sherry
¼ cup vegetable oil
¼ cup chopped fresh parsley
1 small onion, chopped
4 cloves garlic, chopped
2 to 3 habanero chiles, stemmed and
    chopped
3 tablespoons brown sugar
2 teaspoons soy sauce
1 bay leaf
½ teaspoon salt
Freshly ground black pepper

------

1 (3-pound) pork roast

Mojo Sauce

¼ cup peanut or vegetable oil
½ cup chopped green onion, white
    and green parts
6 cloves garlic
2 habanero chiles, stemmed and
    chopped
⅓ cup freshly squeezed orange juice
2 tablespoons freshly squeezed lime
    juice
Salt and freshly ground black pepper

Bolillo (hard rolls)

To make the adobo, place all the ingredients in a blender or food processor and purée until smooth. If you have an injector, fill it with the adobo and inject it into the roast in various places. If you don't have an injector, make shallow slits about 2 inches apart in the roast. Rub the marinade over the meat, and be sure to rub the marinade into the slits. Place the pork and the remaining marinade in a bowl, cover, and marinate in the refrigerator overnight. Remove the pork from the marinade and simmer the marinade for 20 minutes in a pan over medium heat.

Secure the roast on a spit and grill over a medium-hot fire, basting with the marinade, for about 2 hours or until an internal temperature of 155° is reached. If you allow the roast to sit for 10 minutes before carving, the temperature will increase to 160°.

To make the mojo sauce, heat the oil in a sauté pan over medium heat and sauté the onion and garlic until soft. Add the remaining ingredients and simmer for a couple of minutes. Transfer the sautéed ingredients to a blender or food processor and purée until smooth. To serve, carve the roast into thin slices. Split the rolls in half lengthwise, place the meat on the rolls, and top with the mojo sauce. Serve additional mojo on the side.

Seared Chipotle and Garlic Venison

SERVES: 4
HEAT SCALE: Medium

Game is turning up more and more in many fancy restaurants because, like venison, most of it is low in fat and has about half the calories of most cuts of beef, pork, and lamb. All game available from butchers is farm-raised and doesn't taste as "gamey" as wild meat. Because venison is so low in fat, the cook often needs to add oil or fat during the cooking. It is best cooked rare or medium-rare. If you can find it, you can substitute elk for the venison. This dish goes well with steak fries, steamed broccoli, and an elegant semigrilled dessert such as Grilled Peach Halves Stuffed with Cheese and Chipotle Raspberry Sauce (p. 175). That's a double chipotle hit of smoky flavor.

4 dried chipotle chiles	2 teaspoons brown sugar
⅓ cup olive oil	2 teaspoons ground chile de árbol or
½ cup chopped onion	other small, hot red chiles
8 cloves garlic	1 teaspoon Worcestershire sauce
½ cup dry red wine	4 venison steaks or beef steaks, 1
2 tablespoons red wine vinegar	inch thick
2 teaspoons Dijon mustard	

Cover the chipotle chiles with hot water and soak for 30 minutes to soften. Drain and remove the stems and seeds from the chiles.

Heat the oil in a skillet over medium heat. Sauté the onion until soft. Add the garlic and sauté for an additional 2 minutes. Allow to cool.

Place all the ingredients, except the venison, along with the onion-garlic mixture in a blender or food processor and purée until smooth.

Place the meat in a nonreactive pan, cover with the marinade, and marinate, covered, for 2 hours in the refrigerator.

Grill over a medium fire, basting frequently with the marinade, and turning often, for about 16 minutes, until rare or medium-rare (internal temperature at 150°). Slice one of the steaks open to check for doneness, if you wish.

To serve, place the steaks on individual plates.

 # Mayan Achiote-Marinated Pork
Cooked in Banana Leaves and Served with Habanero-Spiced Black Beans *(pictured in photo section)*

SERVES: 4
HEAT SCALE: Hot

This is a pre-Columbian dish and probably the best known of all Yucatan foods. It is called cochinita pibil *in Spanish and was traditionally cooked in the* pib, *the cooking hole, or pit. This was the center of the Mayan community and the place where they did all their cooking, on flat stones over charcoal.*

This variation can be done on a grill and does not require digging a hole in your backyard. Achiote is annatto, which is both a spice and an orange coloring agent, and the paste can be found in Latin—and sometimes Asian—markets. Banana leaves can be found in Asian markets, but you can also use aluminum foil. Epazote is an herb that is always used to flavor the beans in the Yucatán and because of its distinctive flavor, there is really no substitute. So, if you don't have any epazote, just omit it from the recipe.

Achiote Marinade
10 whole black peppercorns
¼ teaspoon cumin seeds
5 cloves garlic
2 habanero chiles, stemmed and
    seeded
3 tablespoons achiote paste
1 teaspoon dried Mexican or other
    oregano
2 bay leaves
⅓ cup freshly squeezed lime juice

2 pounds lean pork, cut into 1½- to
    2-inch cubes
2 large banana leaves, cut into 4 (10-
    inch) squares

3 fresh banana or *guero* chiles,
    stemmed, seeded, and cut into
    strips
1 small red onion, sliced and
    separated into rings
6 to 8 corn tortillas, warmed

Habanero-Spiced Black Beans
1 pound black beans
2 small onions, quartered
4 large cloves garlic
1 tablespoon dried *epazote*
1 habanero chile, stemmed, seeded,
    and chopped

To make the marinade, place the peppercorns and cumin seeds in a spice or coffee grinder and process to a fine powder. In a food processor, combine the powder with the garlic and habanero chiles and process until puréed.

In a small bowl, combine the purée with the achiote, oregano, bay leaves, and lime juice. Place the pork in a large bowl and pour the marinade over the pork. Marinate in the refrigerator overnight or for 24 hours.

Place the beans in a large pot, cover with water and soak overnight.

For each packet, cut 2 pieces of string about 6 inches long. Lay the strings down on a flat surface and place the banana leaf square on top of the strings. Place a fourth of the pork on the leaf and top with one fourth of the banana chiles and onion. Fold the banana leaf over the meat and tie with the strings. Make 4 packets.

Place the packets on the grill over indirect heat and cook for 1½ hours.

To make the beans, bring the pot with the beans to a boil over high heat, decrease the heat slightly to medium-high, and cook for an hour. Add the onions, garlic, *epazote*, and chiles. Simmer over medium-low heat for 1 additional hour or until the beans are tender.

Remove the onion slices from the beans. Drain the beans, capturing the liquid. Mash the beans, adding the cooking water as needed to achieve a smooth consistency.

Place the banana packets on a platter, cut the strings, and uncover the pork. Serve with the warmed tortillas and a bowl of the spiced beans.

VARIATION: Keep the banana leaves whole and make 2 large packets.

Those Are Spitting Words

Many of our familiar grilled-meat dishes have their origin in the Middle East and Central Asia, and involve meat, usually lamb, marinated in oil and spices, then spitted and cooked over hot coals. "Shish kebab" comes from the Turkish; *shish (sis)* means "skewer" and *kebab (kebab, kebap)* means a chunk of meat. In Russian the dish is called "shashlik," in Greek "souvlakia." It is interesting that both "grill" and "skewer" have entered our contemporary vocabulary as unabashedly aggressive metaphors: to "grill" someone means to question relentlessly, to subject him to heat; to "skewer" means to puncture, to defeat, to nail someone to the wall.

—Elisabeth Rozin, *The Universal Kitchen*

Genghis Khan Barbecue

SERVES: 4 to 6
HEAT SCALE: Medium

No, this is not barbecued camel, but you could use it if American markets would only wise up and stock it. ("Special Bactrian Hump, Just $12.95 a Pound!") This Mongol specialty is our take on a nomadic campfire feast and will work fine over a hardwood fire if you want to camp in your backyard. You could, of course, also use your Weber.

The Khan Marinade
2 tablespoons rice wine
1 tablespoon soy sauce
2 tablespoons minced leeks, white
 part only
1 teaspoon sugar
2 teaspoons sesame oil
2 teaspoons minced garlic
3 jalapeño chiles, stemmed, seeded,
 and minced
¼ teaspoon ground white pepper

1½ pounds lamb, sliced 1½ inches
 thick
2 to 3 cups cooked white rice

Chile Garlic Dipping Sauce
1 tablespoon rice wine vinegar, or
 2 tablespoons rice wine
4 red serrano or jalapeño chiles,
 stemmed, seeded, and minced
4 cloves garlic, chopped
1 teaspoon sugar

1 teaspoon peanut oil

Red Wine Chile Dipping Sauce
⅓ cup dry red wine
1 green onion, minced, green and
 white parts
1 jalapeño chile, stemmed, seeded,
 and minced
2 teaspoons chile oil (chiles steeped
 in vegetable oil)
1 clove garlic, minced

The Vegetable Barbecue
12 cremini or button mushrooms
1 leek, cut into 3-inch lengths, then
 into strips, white and green parts
4 green onions, cut into 3-inch
 lengths, white and green parts
1 small bell pepper, stemmed,
 seeded, and thickly sliced
¼ pound edible pea pods
2 jalapeño chiles, stemmed, seeded,
 and cut into strips

To make the marinade, combine all the ingredients in a blender or food processor and purée until smooth. Place the lamb in a glass dish and pour the marinade over it, coating it thoroughly. Marinate the meat for 3 to 4 hours, covered, in the refrigerator.

To make the dipping sauces, combine all the ingredients in two bowls and allow to sit for at least 1 hour to blend the flavors. Place the contents of the bowls in a blender or food processor in two batches and process until smooth. Be sure to rinse out the blender between uses.

Drain the lamb and transfer the leftover marinade to a saucepan. Simmer the marinade over low heat for 20 minutes. Toss the vegetables in the marinade and transfer them to a vegetable-grilling basket.

Over a medium fire, grill the lamb and the vegetables. The lamb should be cooked for 10 to 12 minutes until medium-rare. Cut open a sample to check for doneness. The vegetables should be shaken often and cooked until easily pierced with a knife, about 15 minutes.

Serve the lamb and vegetables with the rice and the dipping sauces on the side. You can also pour the dipping sauces over the entire meal.

VARIATION: Thread the meat and vegetables on skewers to grill.

The Etymology of Barbecue

The most plausible theory states that the word *barbecue* is a derivative of the West Indian term *barbacoa*, which denotes a method of slow-cooking meat over hot coals. *Bon Appetit* magazine blithely informs its readers that the word comes from an extinct tribe in Guyana who enjoyed "cheerfully spit-roasting captured enemies." *The Oxford English Dictionary* traces the word back to Haiti, and others claim (somewhat implausibly) that *barbecue* actually comes from the French phrase *barbe a queue*, meaning "from head to tail." Proponents of this theory point to the whole-hog cooking method espoused by some barbecue chefs. *Tar Heel* magazine posits that the word *barbecue* comes from a nineteenth-century advertisement for a combination whiskey bar, beer hall, pool establishment, and purveyor of roast pig, known as the BAR-BEER-CUE-PIG. The most convincing explanation is that the method of roasting meat over powdery coals was picked up from indigenous peoples in the colonial period, and that *barbacoa* became *barbecue* in the lexicon of early settlers.

Armenian Spiced Lamb Brochettes on Nutty Rice Pilaf

SERVES: 4 to 6
HEAT SCALE: Medium

No matter how you spell it, shisk kebab or sis kebabi, this robust specialty features skewered chunks of meat and onions marinated in oil and spices and then grilled over an open flame. The technique apparently originated in the Caucasus and then spread southward to Mediterranean countries. The meat traditionally used has always been leg of lamb, a meat that seems to be permitted by most major religions. To make a perfect kebab, remove any tough membranes from the meat and cut it across the grain— and don't forget that the meat must be marinated before grilling. Serve the lamb and rice with a salad of tossed greens, ripe olives, and feta cheese.

Cayenne-Infused Meat Marinade

1 teaspoon cumin seeds
⅓ cup olive oil
2 tablespoons freshly squeezed
   lemon juice
1 tablespoon soy sauce
2 tablespoons dry sherry
1 cup finely chopped onion
3 tablespoons finely chopped fresh
   parsley
1 tablespoon peeled and finely
   chopped fresh ginger
2 cloves garlic, minced
2 teaspoons ground cayenne chile
1 teaspoon ground paprika
2 teaspoons chopped fresh oregano
½ teaspoon ground cinnamon
Salt and freshly ground black pepper

The Brochettes

1½ pounds boneless lamb, cut into
   1- to 1½-inch cubes
1 large bell pepper, stemmed,
   seeded, and cut into 1½-inch
   squares
1 small onion, cut into 1½-inch
   squares
12 cherry tomatoes
12 cremini mushrooms, stemmed

Nutty Rice Pilaf

⅛ teaspoon saffron
2 tablespoons olive oil
3 tablespoons blanched almonds
3 tablespoons pistachio nuts
½ cup vermicelli, broken into 1-inch
   pieces
1 cup long-grain rice
2½ cups chicken or beef broth
½ teaspoon ground cayenne chile

To make the marinade, toast the cumin seeds in a dry skillet over medium-low heat until fragrant, taking care that they don't burn. Remove from the heat, allow to cool, and crush. Place all the ingredients for the marinade in a blender or food processor and purée until smooth. Season with salt and pepper.

Reserve 2 teaspoons of the marinade for the rice. Transfer the rest of the marinade to a bowl, add the lamb, toss well to coat, cover, and marinate overnight in the refrigerator, turning occasionally.

To make the pilaf, pour 2 tablespoons of boiling water over the saffron in a cup and let sit for 20 minutes. Heat the oil in a skillet over medium heat, and lightly fry the nuts, stirring constantly, for 2 minutes. Remove the nuts from the oil with a slotted spoon and set aside. Turn heat to low, add the vermicelli to the pan and cook, stirring constantly, until lightly browned, about 2 minutes. Add the rice and stir to coat. Sauté for a couple of minutes or until the kernels are opaque.

Heat the broth with the cayenne over high heat until it boils and pour over the rice mixture. Bring back to a boil while stirring. Decrease the heat to low, and simmer, covered, until the rice is done, about 20 minutes. Fluff with a fork, then add the nuts. The rice can also be baked, covered, in a 325° oven for 40 minutes.

To make the brochettes, blanch the bell pepper and the onions in boiling water for 2 minutes, remove with a slotted spoon, and run under cold water. Remove the lamb from the marinade and reserve the marinade. Thread the meat on skewers, alternating with the pepper, onion, tomatoes and mushrooms. Brush with the reserved marinade.

Grill over a medium-hot fire until medium-rare, about 15 minutes. Baste occasionally with the marinade. Cut a sample of the meat to check for doneness.

Place a scoop of the pilaf on individual plates, divide the brochettes equally and arrange on the pilaf.

Pita Pockets Stuffed with Harissa-Spiced Moroccan Lamb Brochettes

SERVES: 4
HEAT SCALE: Hot

Nancy learned how to make these brochettes while traveling through Morocco in a VW bus in the '70s. She and Jeff would find small, homemade charcoal braziers by the side of the road and a vendor would sell them the brochettes by the skewer and served in flat Arab bread. After hanging around enough vendors, Nancy witnessed the entire spicing and grilling process. Harissa is a fiery pepper paste that is used as an ingredient in couscous and grilled dishes, or as a condiment served on the side of a Moroccan meal. Serve the pitas with cold artichokes or our Grilled Artichokes (p. 164).

Moroccan Harissa
¼ cup small, dried hot chiles such as piquín, or 10 dried red New Mexican chiles, stemmed and seeded
2 large pimientos, fresh, canned or bottled, roasted and chopped
2 tablespoons plus ¼ cup olive oil
5 cloves garlic
1 teaspoon ground cumin
1 teaspoon ground coriander
1 teaspoon ground caraway
1 tablespoon chopped fresh parsley

2 tablespoons freshly squeezed lemon juice
1 teaspoon freshly ground black pepper
1½ pounds boneless lamb, cut into 1-inch cubes

4 pieces of pita bread
Chopped cucumber, for garnish
Chopped onion, for garnish
Chopped tomatoes, for garnish
Shredded lettuce, for garnish

Cover the chiles with hot water and let sit for 20 minutes, until softened. Drain the chiles. Place all of the harissa ingredients, except ¼ cup olive oil, in a blender or food processor and purée until smooth. With the motor running, add the remaining oil in a steady stream to form a thick sauce.

Put aside a small amount of harissa. In a plastic bag, marinate the lamb in the rest of the harissa for 3 hours to overnight in the refrigerator.

Bring the meat to room temperature, thread the cubes on skewers, and grill over a medium-hot fire for about 15 minutes, turning often.

Remove the meat from the skewers and serve the meat in the pita bread with a little reserved harissa, garnished with cucumber, onion, tomato, and lettuce.

The Hamburger Museum

In a tribute to burgers of all kinds—grilled or not—Harry Sperl of Daytona Beach, Florida has assembled more than 500 different artifacts that depict hamburgers. They include piggy banks, biscuit jars, clocks, hats, trays, erasers, badges, magnets, music boxes, glasses, cups, bowls, stuffed toys, calendars, and postcards. The two prize pieces are a hamburger waterbed with a sesame seed-covered spread and matching pillows and a Harley motorcycle that is customized as a giant hamburger replica. Hamburger lovers should surf on over to www.burgerweb. com for a complete description of the museum and its contents.

SIX

Fired-Up American BBQ Classics

WELCOME to the Regional Barbecue Wars. For centuries now, the rival factions have been firing off their best barbecues at each other, but at least they do it in a fairly civilized manner: with rival pits at cook-offs big and small. The big battles are the East versus the West in North Carolina, but don't forget about North Carolina pitted (ha, ha) against South Carolina. Georgia versus Alabama sounds like a football rivalry—and it is—but it also extends to BBQ. The biggest cook-off conflict has Memphis-in-May against the American Royal in Kansas City. And of course, there's Texas versus Everyone Else. The minor skirmishes include beef versus pork, ribs versus brisket, pulled versus chopped pork, and mustard versus ketchup as a base for sauces. Whew. It's downright contentious on all levels in the barbecue battles.

In the midst of all this conflict, a few food historians have noticed a common denominator in regional barbecue—the overwhelming tendency to use chile peppers to spice up the smoked meats. So traditional American regional barbecue is true fiery food, with chile peppers appearing in rubs, sops, marinades, and barbecue sauces from all over the country.

Despite the tradition of chiles in barbecue, our critics might complain that we have altered hallowed, sacred, and traditional regional recipes by spicing them up too much. To counter that charge, we reply that home cooks are not stupid. By reading the recipe and noting the heat scale before starting, you can easily asjust the amount of chile in the recipe to taste.

We'd like to remind the cook that smoking meats is a very simple method of cooking and the variations are limited to the type of wood used as well as the different rubs, marinades, mops, and finishing sauces applied to the meat. The basic technique of, say, smoking pork ribs, remains the same whether you're in Memphis, Kansas City, or North Carolina. It is the flavorings added to the smoking process that make the difference, and if you want to use a Memphis rub with a Kansas City–style barbecue sauce, or a North Carolina sauce over brisket, be our guest.

Rich Davis and Shifra Stein's
Ten Commandments of Barbecue

1   Smoke It Slow and Keep the Fire Low.

2. Use High Heat Only When Grilling or Searing.

3. Don't Trim the Fat off Brisket and Ribs before Smoking.

4. Remember that Traditionally Barbecued Meats Are Well Done.

5. Don't Confuse Grilling with Barbecuing.

6. Consider the Wind and the Outdoor Temperature.

7. Learn When to Use Sauces.

8. Make the Best Use of Wood.

9. Use Charcoal Briquets Properly.

10. Bring Meat to Room Temperature before Cooking.

from *Wild about Kansas City Barbecue*

Texas Beef Brisket, New Mexico–Style

SERVES: 15 to 20
HEAT SCALE: Medium

Okay, okay, we borrowed a Texas technique and changed the rub to reflect our chile-head tastes. For years we have been perfecting recipes using a smoker known as an Oklahoma Joe's. It is a horizontal, cylindrical smoker about 3½ half feet long and about 14 inches in diameter. It has an attached, dropped firebox that allows smoking with fairly cool smoke because the fire is separated from the smoking area. Because smoking is so time consuming, it makes sense to smoke several things at once. In addition to brisket, we also smoke a turkey breast (see recipe, p. 123). Some cooks use the basting sauce as a mop during the smoking process and eliminate the long marinade at the end of smoking. Leftovers, if there are any, make the best barbecue sandwiches when served on a crusty hard roll with your choice of sauce from Chapter 3.

1 (9- to 10-pound) "packer-trimmed" brisket	1 tablespoon ground cayenne chile
½ cup freshly squeezed lemon juice	2 tablespoons freshly ground black pepper
2 cups ground red mild New Mexican chile	¼ cup garlic powder
	Brisket Basting Sauce (p. 33)

Thoroughly coat all surfaces of the brisket with lemon juice, and rub in well. Combine the chile, cayenne, black pepper, and garlic powder in a bowl, and sprinkle generously all over the brisket, rubbing it in well. Make sure that the brisket is entirely covered. Marinate at room temperature for at least an hour before smoking.

To smoke the brisket, build a hardwood fire in the fire box using pecan, oak, or any fruit wood. When the fire is smoking nicely, place the brisket on the rack fat side up to let gravity and nature do the basting. Place the brisket as far from the heat source as possible, and close the smoker. During the smoking, do nothing to the brisket. The smoking will take approximately 8 hours at 200° smoke temperature. This means a lot of beer will be consumed while you wait and tend the fire.

After the brisket has finished smoking, remove it from the smoker, slather it generously with basting sauce, wrap it tightly in aluminum foil, and return it to the smoker. Close off all of the air supplies to the fire, and allow the meat to "set" in the pit for about 2 hours.

Slice the brisket against the grain and arrange on a large platter. Serve with additional basting sauce on the side and cold beers.

VARIATION: A great sandwich can be made with French rolls, brisket, and sliced onions, covered with the Brisket Basting Sauce.

 ## Texas Fajitas

SERVES: 6 to 8
HEAT SCALE: Mild to Medium

There is no such thing as a chicken or tofu fajita because the word refers specifically to skirt steak that is marinated and grilled. This is actually a simple recipe to prepare, and it works best when grilled over mesquite wood or natural charcoal with mesquite chips. The technique known as smoke-grilling is perfect for this meat, and flank steak can be substituted for the skirt steak. Tradition holds that fajitas were first perfected in south Texas in the 1960s and quickly became a staple in Mexican restaurants—and others— north of the border. It is a classic example of combining several methods to make tough meat more palatable: Marinate it, grill it, and slice it thinly against the grain.

Jalapeño Marinade
⅓ cup freshly squeezed lime juice
⅓ cup soy sauce
⅓ cup red wine
2 cloves garlic, minced
2 tablespoons vegetable oil
3 jalapeño chiles, stemmed, seeded, and minced

2 pounds skirt steak

8 flour tortillas
Grated Monterey Jack and Cheddar cheeses
Sour cream
Guacamole (p. 55)
Grilled onions (see p. 59)
Texas Chilipiquín Barbecue Sauce (p. 35)
Pico de Gallo (p. 109)
Commercial hot sauce (optional)

To make the marinade, combine the ingredients in a bowl and mix well. Place the steak in a glass dish and pour the marinade over it. Cover and marinate in the refrigerator overnight.

Grill the steak over a hot fire until medium-rare, 10 to 15 minutes, or if you can measure the temperature with a probe, to 150° internal temperature. You can also check for doneness by cutting into the steak. Remove the steak from the grill and slice thinly against the grain.

Quickly heat each tortilla on the grill. Serve the sliced steak wrapped in a tortilla and topped with your choice of condiments among the cheese, sour cream, guacamole, grilled onions, barbecue sauce, pico de gallo, and hot sauce.

VARIATION: Sauté onions, bell peppers, chiles, and tomato wedges in hot oil as a topping for fajitas.

 ## Memphis Baby Back Ribs

SERVES: 4
HEAT SCALE: Medium

This particular specialty can be smoked or smoke-grilled. It typifies the Memphis approach to cooking ribs—a double whammy of spices and sauce. As usual, watch for burning as the finishing sauce has a bit of sugar in the tomato. Why not serve these delicious ribs with traditional potato salad, coleslaw, and pickled peppers? Remember that the meat on smoked ribs looks pink, but that's because of a chemical reaction with the smoke, not because the ribs aren't really done. It is difficult to take the temperature of the ribs because of the bones, so some instinctive cooking is required here.

1 cup Memphis Rib Rub (p. 30)
3 slabs baby back ribs, about
    4 pounds total

1 cup Memphis-Style Finishing Sauce
    (p. 42)

In a large, shallow pan, pour the rub over the ribs and massage into the meat on both sides. Cover and refrigerate for 4 hours. Remove the ribs from the refrigerator and bring to room temperature.

The Politically Correct Southern Pig

"But only in the South does the slow cooking of meat over the smoke of hardwood embers assume a level of ritual and tradition usually associated with Masonic orders." John Shelton Reed, a professional Dixieologist at the University of North Carolina, put it well when he suggested that since the Rebel flag had become too controversial, we replace it with a symbol that all Southerners could support: a neon pig.

—Jim Auchmutey, "A Southern View on Barbecue"

If smoke-grilling the ribs, build a fire that is 300 to 350°. Cook the ribs, covered, for 1 hour, turning often. Smoke-grill, basting the finishing sauce on the ribs with a brush, for another 30 minutes.

If smoking the ribs, maintain the smoke at 200 to 220° and smoke for 2 hours. Brush the finishing sauce over the ribs several times during the last hour of smoking, and turn the ribs occasionally.

Remove the ribs from the grill or smoker, slice into individual ribs, and pile them up on a platter. Serve with additional finishing sauce on the side.

 # Kansas City Long-Ends

SERVES: 4 to 6
HEAT SCALE: Medium

Long-ends are the lean, thin bones of spareribs, while short-ends are the shorter, fatter, meatier hind sections. The combination of the rub and finishing sauce is traditional in Kansas City–style barbecue. The sauce is sometimes slathered over the ribs during the last half hour of smoking and is always served on the side. Why not serve these ribs with french fries, corn-on-the-cob, and spicy baked beans, with mixed grilled fruits (see sidebar, p. 170) for dessert?

Kansas City Dry Rub (p. 32)

6 to 8 pounds pork spareribs, long
ends only

Kansas City–Style Barbecue Sauce
(40)

Place the rub in a shaker. Sprinkle evenly over the ribs and let them marinate for 2 hours at room temperature or overnight in the refrigerator.

Prepare a fire and place the ribs on racks in the smoker. Smoke at approximately 200° for 4 hours. If desired, baste with the sauce during the last ½ hour of smoking.

Remove the ribs from the smoker, cut into individual ribs, and pile on a platter with the sauce served in a bowl on the side.

Smoked Prime Ribs of Beef

SERVES: 4

HEAT SCALE: Medium

We cannot eliminate beef from the rib race. It is smoked everywhere in the U.S., but the only area claiming it as the main barbecue meat is Texas—and that's mostly brisket and skirt steak. Buy a large prime rib roast and cut away the center. Then slice the rib-less roast into rib eye steaks to use in the steak recipes in Chapter 5. Then slice the ribs apart so that more smoke will reach them. Serve these ribs with Chile-Grilled Potato Wedges (p. 68), corn on the cob, and buttermilk biscuits.

8 large prime ribs

⅔ cup Genuine, Authentic, South-of-
the-Border Chile Rub (p. 32) or
other rub from chapter 3

Smokin' Peachy Barbecue Sauce
(p. 39), or other barbecue sauce
from chapter 3

Trim excess fat off the ribs. Cover with the rub and massage the rub into the meat. Cover and let stand at room temperature for 1 hour.

Build a fire in the smoker and bring the smoke to 200 to 220°. Place the ribs on the grill or on racks and smoke for 4½ hours, turning occasionally.

Brush the ribs all over with barbecue sauce ½ hour before you remove the ribs from the smoker.

Remove the ribs from the smoker and arrange on a platter. Serve with additional sauce on the side.

 # Carolina Pulled Pork Sandwiches with Coleslaw   *(pictured in photo section)*

SERVES: 6 to 8
HEAT SCALE: Mild

Notice that we have not limited this recipe to the "southeastern corner of western North Carolina," but rather have made a universal Carolina recipe that you can sauce up with two or three styles of Carolina BBQ sauces in chapter 3. Even the coleslaw can go north or south. There is a minor debate about whether or not to use a rub, with purists generally preferring to salt the pork roast—a practice most smoking chefs don't approve of. If you wish to use a rub, use the Memphis Rib Rub (p. 30), which is quite similar to Carolina rubs.

Pulled Pork Sandwiches
Memphis Rib Rub (p. 30) (optional)
1 (3- to 4-pound) Boston Butt pork
   roast
6 to 8 Kaiser rolls

Carolina Coleslaw
3 cups shredded cabbage
1 small green bell pepper, thinly
   sliced
¼ cup thinly sliced onion

Slaw Dressing
3 tablespoons cider vinegar
4 teaspoons sugar
1 tablespoon vegetable oil
1 teaspoon Dijon mustard
½ teaspoon celery seeds
Salt and freshly ground black pepper

Sauces
North Carolina Barbecue Sauce
   (p. 41)
South Carolina Mustard Sauce (p. 41)

Sprinkle the rub thickly over the roast and allow to sit, covered and refrigerated, for 3 hours. Start a fire and place the roast in the smoker on a rack. Place a drip pan beneath the grill, as this roast will drip a lot of fat. Smoke

Is This Why Georgia and South Carolina BBQ Sauces Have Mustard in Them Today?

One of the most popular early Southern cookbooks was *Mrs. Hill's New Cook Book*, which was published in 1867. In it, Annabella P. Hill shared her recipe for "Sauce for Barbecues," a sauce that food historian Damon Fowler noted "was the Georgia classic until well into this century, and it is still favored in some parts of the state. Its advantage over modern sweet tomato sauce is that it is less likely to burn.

Sauce for barbecues: Melt half a pound of butter; stir into it a large tablespoon of mustard, half a teaspoon of red pepper and one of black, salt to taste; and add vinegar until the sauce has a strong acid taste. The quantity of the vinegar needed will depend upon the strength of it. As soon as the meat becomes hot, begin to baste, and continue basting frequently until it is done. Pour over meat any sauce that remains."

the roast with 200° smoke for 4 or more hours, until it is falling off the bone, or until the internal temperature reaches 170°.

To make the coleslaw, mix together the salad ingredients in a bowl.

To make the dressing, combine all the ingredients in another bowl. Pour the dressing over the salad and mix well. Cover and refrigerate for 2 hours.

Remove the roast from the smoker, transfer it to a cutting board, and allow it to sit for 20 minutes. With your fingers, remove any skin and fat from the roast. Pull the pork into thin pieces, about 1½ inches long. This is slippery work and tedious, so if you get frustrated, take out a knife and chop the pork into ½-inch pieces. Then change the name of this recipe to Carolina Chopped Pork Sandwiches.

To serve, place the pork on the buns, spread the sauce of choice over the pork, and then add coleslaw to taste.

Kentucky Barbecued Lamb

SERVES: 8 to 10
HEAT SCALE: Mild

To our knowledge, there are two main areas in the States where lamb and goat are really popular: Kentucky and the true Southwest, meaning west and south Texas, New Mexico, Arizona, and sometimes Colorado and southern California. In the Southwest, the cabrito *or young goat is barbecued pit-style, with limited smoke and no flame. In Kentucky, both lamb and mutton are celebrated barbecue meats, with a festival tradition that dates back to 1834. They still reign supreme today at the Owensboro Bar-B-Q Championship. This barbecue is unusual in that the lamb is first marinated in what's locally called a "dip," then rubbed with a spice mixture. Serve with grilled green tomatoes, black-eyed peas, and of course, a cool mint julep.*

Lamb "Dip" or Marinade
1 cup Worcestershire sauce
1 cup apple cider vinegar
½ cup firmly packed brown sugar
¼ cup minced onion
1 teaspoon ground allspice
1 teaspoon salt
¼ cup freshly squeezed lime juice
2 tablespoons freshy ground black
    pepper
2 tablespoons minced garlic
1 quart water

Kentucky Lamb Rub
¼ cup firmly packed brown sugar
2 tablespoons freshly ground black
    pepper
2 tablespoons dried onion flakes
1 tablespoon garlic powder
2 teaspoons commercial chili powder
1 teaspoon ground allspice

1 (4- to 5-pound) leg of lamb

To make the "dip," combine all the ingredients in a large pot over high heat and bring to a boil. Decrease the heat to medium and simmer for 45 minutes. Remove from the heat and allow to cool.

Place the lamb in a large plastic bag or nonreactive container, pour the marinade into the bag, shake to coat the meat, and refrigerate for 12 to 24 hours.

Remove the lamb from the marinade and bring to room temperature.

Heat the remaining marinade in a saucepan over medium heat and simmer for 20 minutes. Start a fire in the smoker and bring the smoke to 200 to 220°.

To make the rub, mix all the ingredients together in a bowl. Spread the rub evenly over the lamb. Place the lamb on a rack in the smoker and smoke for 6 to 7 hours, until the internal temperature is 170° for well-done. Remove the lamb from the smoker and either pull it or slice it and place on a large platter. Pour some of the remaining marinade over the lamb and serve the rest on the side.

 ## Barbecued Goat, Shepherd-Style

SERVES: 20 or more
HEAT SCALE: Varies

Known in the Southwest as cabrito al pastor, *barbecued young goat, or kid, is a spring tradition that can be duplicated in a grill with a spit or in a smoker. The biggest problem is going to be finding a young, tender 12- to 15-pound goat. You may have to search out butchers, farmers, or Hispanic markets. You can also substitute a large leg of lamb if you can't find the young goat, and smoke it for 30 minutes a pound to an internal temperature of 150°.*

Getting Your Goat in Texas

Because of the culinary influence from northern Mexico, particularly the state of Nuevo León, goat has always been a popular barbecue meat in Texas. This is particularly true for *cabrito*, the young, milk-fed goat with flesh unsullied by eating grass, that is usually slaughtered at age one month. Perhaps the biggest goat celebration in Texas is the World Championship Barbecue Goat Cook-Off, held every Labor Day since 1974 in Brady. In addition to competition cooks from around the country smoking up the town, the locals smoke as many as 150 goats to serve to the general public.

So It's More than Just a Cult, Anyway

Barbecue is like religion: first, because it can make you swoon in jubilation; and second, because it has so many different sects. There are true believers who are convinced that their kind of barbecue is the *only* good and true one, and that people who use an unorthodox type of wood for their fire, or make sauce a little differently, are heretics.

—Jane and Michael Stern, *Way Out West*

Genuine, Authentic South-of-the-Border Chile Rub (p. 32)
1 (12-pound) young goat, cleaned (ask your butcher to do this for you)
Barbecue sauce of choice, such as Texas Chilipiquín Barbecue Sauce (p. 35), Smokin' Peachy Barbecue Sauce (p. 39), or Chipotle BBQ Sauce (p. 36)

Flour or corn tortillas
Guacamole (p. 55)
Salsa of choice, such as Smoked Fruit Salsa (p. 43)

Sprinkle the rub all over the goat and rub it in thoroughly. If grilling the goat, build a mesquite wood fire in a large barbecue with a spit, or use natural charcoal and mesquite chips. Arrange the goat on a spit about 1 foot above the coals. You can use a motor to turn the spit, or turn it manually every 10 or 15 minutes. Cook until the internal temperature reaches 170°, for well-done.

If smoking the goat, place the goat on a rack in the smoker with the smoke from pecan, oak, or fruitwood at 200 to 220°. Smoke for about 1 hour per pound, or until the internal temperature reaches 180°.

To serve, slice the *cabrito* thinly and top with barbecue sauce. Serve with the tortillas, guacamole, and salsa on the side, or make tacos topped with the salsa.

Grilled Crab-Stuffed Cherry Peppers (p. 58), Spice Islands Coconut-Chile Pork Kebabs with Sambal Marinade (p. 49), and Berbere Kifto (p. 53)

Mayan Achiote-Marinated Pork Cooked in Banana Leaves served with Habanero Spiced Black Beans (p. 80)

Hoisin Beef Ribs (p. 66)

Carolina Pulled Pork Sandwiches with Coleslaw (p. 96)

Habanero-Marinated and Pecan-Smoked Quail (p. 128)
and Grilled Spring Asparagus with Spicy Lemon Mop (p. 167)

*Gingered and Grilled Shrimp Salad
with Crispy Red Chile-Dusted Eggroll Strips (p. 147)*

Grilled Corn with African Nitir Kebe (p. 159) and Mixed Mediterranean Herbed Vegetables with Penne Pasta and Feta Cheese (p. 154)

*Grilled Peach Halves Stuffed with Cheese
and Chipotle Raspberry Purée (p. 175)*

—*The Expert Pitman Protests*—
On Boiling Ribs Before Barbecuing Them

Yeah, you can boil them. Let me tell you, if you do, also buy a pack of noodles. Then when you take the meat out, throw the noodles in so you'll at least have some noodles to eat because you just cooked the best part off the meat.

—Luscious "The King" Newsome

 # Southern Hot Links

SERVES: 10
HEAT SCALE: Medium

Here is our recipe for a typically Southern sausage made with ground pork and lamb. For this recipe you will need a meat grinder with a sausage funnel, a tube that fits over the end of the grinder for filling sausage casings. You can also use a stand mixer with a sausage stuffer attachment. When stuffing, fill the casings until the sausage segments are about 4 inches long, then twist the casing and tie the sausages off with string. Then cut the extra casing off with scissors. Serve the links on buns with raw onions and barbecue sauce, with macaroni salad and baked beans on the side.

2 pounds ground pork, shoulder cut preferred
2 pounds ground beef, round steak preferred
2 teaspoons crushed red chile (piquín for hot, New Mexican for mild)
2 teaspoons paprika
2 teaspoons dried sage
2 teaspoons dried oregano
2 teaspoons dried basil
1 teaspoon ground cumin
1 teaspoon aniseed
10 to 12 sausage casings
10 hot dog buns
Chopped onion, for garnish
Barbecue sauce of choice, such as North Carolina Barbecue Sauce (p. 41)

In a bowl, combine all ingredients except the casings, the chopped onions, and the barbecue sauce and mix well. Using a meat grinder with a stuffing

It's Sorta Like Turkey and Thanksgiving

Six miles of roast pig and that in New York City alone; and roast pig in every other city, town, hamlet, and village in the Union. What association can there be between roast pig and independence?

—Captain Frederick Marryat,
reporting on a 4th of July celebration during a visit to America in the 1830s

attachment, grind the mixture, stuff the sausage casings, and tie them off with string. Build a fire in the smoker, place the sausages on the grill in the smoker, and smoke at 200 to 220° for about 3 hours, or until the internal temperature reaches 170°.

Serve the hot links on a bun with the chopped onions and a barbecue sauce of choice.

 ## Honey and Chile-Glazed Smoked Ham

SERVES: 20
HEAT SCALE: Medium

Some specialty hams, like those from around Smithfield, Virginia, take months and months to cure and smoke, which is way too long to approximate in the home smoker. Most commercial hams found in supermarkets are cured and cooked, but not smoked. You can, however, prepare a mighty tasty smoked ham in just a few hours in the smoker by purchasing a cooked ham and smoking it yourself. Serve with scalloped potatoes, fresh peas, and hot corn bread.

1 (10-pound) cooked ham
Ragin' Cajun Rub (p. 30)
1 cup honey
½ cup soy sauce

¼ cup ground New Mexican red
    chile
South Carolina Mustard Sauce (p. 41)

Oh, Those Tarheel Pig Lovers

William Byrd, in his eighteenth century book writings, *The Secret History of the Dividing Line Betwixt Virginia and North Carolina*, has some pretty snippy things to say about some Southerners' predilection for pork. He writes that hog meat was ". . . the staple commodity of North Carolina . . . and with pitch and tar makes up the whole of their traffic . . . these people live so much upon swine's flesh that it don't only incline them to the yaws, and consequently to the . . . [loss] of their noses, but makes them likewise extremely hoggish in their temper, and many of them seem to grunt rather than speak in their ordinary conversation."

"Yaws," of course, is an infectious tropical disease closely related to syphilis. Perhaps because of natives like Byrd, Virginia is frequently considered beyond the parameters of the "barbecue belt."

—Laura Dove, "BBQ—A Southern Cultural Icon."

Wash the ham in cold water and pat dry. Spread the rub thoroughly over the ham, place the ham in a plastic bag, and refrigerate 12 hours or preferably overnight.

Prepare a fire in the smoker with a hardwood such as oak and bring the smoke to 200 to 220°. Smoke the ham for 4 hours.

In a bowl, combine the honey, soy sauce, and chile and mix well. Brush the glaze over the ham and return it to the smoker for another hour, applying the glaze three more times. Remove the ham from the smoker and let it sit for 15 minutes.

To serve, carve the ham on a platter. Pour some of the mustard sauce over the top and serve the remainder of the sauce on the side.

SEVEN

Powerful Poultry
plus a Rather Pungent Ostrich

TEXANS LOVE BRISKET, Carolinians love pork, and Kentuckians love mutton. But everyone loves barbecued chicken despite the fact that there seems to be no cook-off in the United States devoted to the bird. Now you'd think that a chicken-producing state like Maryland or Delaware would have a barbecued chicken cook-off, but we have not been able to locate one—a fowl development. But chickens appear and are judged at cook-offs everywhere, and they're not deep-fried. They're grilled, smoke-grilled, or just plain smoked. This is because if any mass-produced food needs chiles, smoke, and fire, it's chicken.

There are certain meats, like an aged filet mignon, that can be grilled as is with no rub, marinade, or finishing sauce, and it will be superb. But bland chicken needs some help, as does other poultry, such as turkey, Cornish game hens, and guinea hens. In outdoor cooking, chicken is usually grilled and turkey smoked, but a simple smoked and spiced chicken is much tastier than the usual kitchen-cooked bird. Duck is perhaps the most flavorful bird for the smoker or grill, but for some reason it is rarely used.

> Grilled chicken ranks among the world's most popular barbecue. The diversity of its preparation is limited only by the imagination of the world's grill jockeys.
>
> —Steven Raichlen, *The Barbecue Bible*

There has been a lot of interest lately in specialty birds like ostrich and emu. They are very lean and need the assistance of marinades and sauces to make them palatable on the grill. They are also rather expensive, assuming you can find them. We like them but doubt that they will be overwhelmingly popular for smoking and grilling.

Nancy notes that the recipes in this chapter work well with all types of birds, so feel free, to interchange all the poultry, but remember to consider the size of the bird or pieces of bird that you are working with. Obviously a ten-pound turkey will take longer to cook than a three-pound chicken. And some birds have more fat than others, so it is important with poultry to grill it slowly and watch it carefully so that the fatty skin doesn't flare up and burn. The food police will order you to remove all the skin from poultry before grilling it, but we buck that trend because of one simple reason: As bland as chicken is, once it's treated with the right marinade and grilling sauces and grilled correctly, there are few things better tasting in the world than a perfect, crispy piece of chicken skin. Dave's mom, Barbara, insisted on eating *only* the skin of grilled chicken, provided that Dick DeWitt didn't burn it.

One of Nancy's favorite techniques is popular in the eastern Caribbean and consists of spreading marinades or rubs under the skin as well as over it. She says that the chicken doesn't burn as easily and that the grilling "bastes the flavors into the meat." It takes a little practice so you don't get the skin completely separated from the meat, but it's worth the effort.

Southwestern Grilled Chicken Caesar Salad with Chile-Dusted Croutons

SERVES: 4
HEAT SCALE: Medium

The Caesar salad was invented in Tijuana, Mexico, so it has some south-of-the-border roots. Here we give it a Southwestern twist by taking it outside on the grill for a terrific summer entrée. Shaved Parmesan cheese as a garnish is a better presentation than just grated cheese. To shave cheese, use a vegetable peeler to make inch-wide shavings, then refrigerate until ready to serve. Please note that the food police discourage the consumption of raw eggs.

Southwestern Chicken

2 whole boneless, skinless chicken
   breasts
Olive oil
2 tablespoons Genuine, Authentic
   South-of-the-Border Chile Rub
   (p. 32)

Chile-Dusted Croutons

⅓ cup olive oil
3 cloves garlic, minced
1 tablespoon ground Chimayo chile
   or red New Mexican chile
½ teaspoon garlic salt
5 slices French or Italian bread, cut
   into ½-inch cubes

Southwestern Caesar Dressing

2 egg yolks
¼ cup grated Parmesan cheese
1 teaspoon anchovy paste
2 teaspoons Dijon mustard
1 tablespoon freshly squeezed lemon
   juice
½ cup red wine vinegar
1½ cups olive oil
2 tablespoons ground Chimayo chile
   or red New Mexico chile
¼ teaspoon cumin seeds
Freshly ground black pepper

The Salad

Inner leaves of romaine lettuce, torn
   into 2-inch pieces (6 to 8 cups)
2 thin slices red onion, separated into
   rings
⅓ cup shaved Parmesan cheese

Brush the chicken with a little olive oil and sprinkle with the rub. Allow the chicken to marinate at room temperature for 30 minutes to an hour.

To prepare the croutons, preheat the oven to 350°. In a small bowl, mix together the olive oil, garlic, chile, and garlic salt. Toss with the bread cubes until thoroughly coated. Spread on a baking sheet and toast in the oven for 10 minutes.

To make the dressing, in a bowl, whisk together the egg yolks, cheese, anchovy paste, and mustard. Add the lemon juice and blend well. While whisking, slowly add the vinegar and then the olive oil, a little at a time. Whisk in the chile, cumin, and black pepper. Refrigerate until ready to serve. Taste and adjust the dressing, adding more vinegar if you like it more tart, more oil if you prefer it less tart, more chile for heat, or more anchovies for saltiness.

Grill the chicken over a medium-hot fire until cooked through, about 30 minutes, or until the internal temperature reaches 160°, for medium. Remove the chicken from the grill and cut it crosswise into thin slices.

To assemble the salad, toss the lettuce with some of the dressing until coated but not saturated. Divide the lettuce on individual chilled plates. Top with the onion, chicken, and croutons. Garnish with the shaved Parmesan and serve.

Grilled Split Thai Chicken with Fiery Red Chile Sauce

SERVES: 4
HEAT SCALE: Hot

Chickens grilled in this way are very popular throughout Thailand, where they're sold in village bus stations, portable food stands, at the beach, or anywhere else. The Thais use bamboo skewers, but metal ones work fine. The skewers keep the chicken flat as it cooks on the grill. You will notice that the chicken is doubly spiced, like American barbecue, but much hotter. Those Thais like their food pungent! The chiles traditionally used are prik kee nu, with medium-hot, cayenne-like, bright red pods. To make a Thai-style picnic, serve the chicken with Asian Chile Slaw (p. 138), and fresh tropical fruit such as pineapple or mango.

Thai Seasoning Paste
12 large cloves garlic, chopped
½ cup chopped shallots
¼ cup peeled and chopped fresh ginger
¼ cup fish sauce or soy sauce
4 stalks lemongrass, peeled to reveal soft inner root and lower stem, chopped
8 to 10 red Thai chiles (*prik kee nu)* or 4 red jalapeño chiles, stemmed and seeded

1 (3- to 3 ½-pound) chicken

Fiery Red Chile Sauce
4 red Thai or red jalapeño chiles, stemmed, seeded, and chopped
3 dried red New Mexican chiles, stemmed and seeded
1 tablespoon peeled and chopped fresh ginger
4 cloves garlic
¾ cup water
½ cup distilled vinegar
2 tablespoons sugar
2 tablespoons chopped fresh Thai basil
Salt

Our Favorite Names of Barbecue Cook-off Teams, Part 2

The Grate Pretenders

Dr. Frank 'n' Swine

Asleep at the Grill

Cayenne Social Club

Swine Flew

Slaughterhouse Five

Aporkalypse Now

To make the paste, place all the ingredients in a food processor or blender and process to a thick paste.

To prepare the chicken, use poultry shears or a heavy knife to cut down both sides of the backbone and cut the chicken in half. Remove the backbone and place the chicken on a cutting board skin side up. Press hard on the breastbone to break it and flatten the bird.

Loosen the skin and rub the paste on the whole chicken, over and under the skin.

Take the skewers and force one through the thigh perpendicular to the bone, just above the drumstick, into the breast, and out through the middle joint of the wing. Repeat for the other side of the chicken.

To prepare the sauce, soak the dried chiles in hot water to soften for about 20 minutes. Drain and chop the chiles. In a blender or food processor place the chiles, ginger, garlic, and water and process until almost puréed, but still coarse. Place in a saucepan with the vinegar and sugar. Cook about 10 minutes over medium heat until reduced by half, transfer to a bowl, and add basil and salt to taste. Stir well.

Place the skewers on the grill over a medium-hot fire. Grill slowly, turning as needed to brown evenly, for about 30 minutes, or until the internal temperature of the chicken is 160° for medium.

Cut the chicken into serving pieces and arrange on a platter. Serve the chile sauce in small bowls.

Mexican Chile-Rubbed Rotisserie Chicken with Frijoles Borrachos and Pico de Gallo Salsa

SERVES: 4 to 6
HEAT SCALE: Medium

Nancy made dozens of attempts to extract the recipe for this classic Mexican chicken from vendors all over Mexico, but they stonewalled her. When she asked what rub was used, they would answer only: "Chile and herbs." But she persisted and with some careful spying deduced this recipe. This is the chicken sold in little stalls in the mercados, in small restaurants on the streets, and even in grocery stores. The meat is placed in tortillas and topped with pico de gallo salsa. The drunken beans (frijoles borrachos) are usually served on the side, but if you want to put them in your taco, we won't call the food police.

Frijoles Borrachos
2 cups pinto beans, sorted and rinsed
   clean
4 jalapeño chiles, stemmed, seeded,
   and cut into strips
1 small onion, cut into wedges
1 strip of bacon, cut into pieces
1 (12-ounce) can Mexican beer
Salt

Pico de Gallo Salsa
6 jalapeño or serrano chiles,
   stemmed, seeded, and finely
   chopped
2 tomatoes, finely chopped
1 small onion, finely chopped
2 tablespoons finely chopped fresh
   cilantro

3 tablespoons vegetable oil
2 to 3 tablespoons red wine vinegar
Salt
12 corn tortillas

---

1 (3½- to 4-pound) chicken
4 large guajillo or dried red New
   Mexican chiles, stemmed and
   seeded
4 chiles de árbol, stemmed and
   seeded
1 teaspoon dried Mexican or
   domestic oregano
2 to 3 teaspoons garlic salt
2 Mexican limes, halved
6 cloves garlic, cut into large pieces
   or slices

To make the beans, combine all the ingredients except the salt in a large pot. Cover with water and let sit overnight in the refrigerator.

To make the salsa, combine all the ingredients in a bowl and let stand for at least 1 hour to allow the flavors to blend.

Clean the chicken and pat dry. Place the dried chiles and oregano in a spice grinder and process to a fine powder. Sprinkle the inside of the chicken with the garlic salt. Rub the outside of the chicken with the lime juice and then the garlic. Coat with the chile mixture, put the chicken on a spit. Place the spit on the rotisserie over a medium fire and grill for about 1 hour, or until the internal temperature in the thigh of the chicken is 165° for medium. Remove the chicken from the spit and let it sit for 10 minutes before carving.

While the chicken is grilling, drain the beans, reserving the water. Place the beans along with the chiles, onion, and bacon in a large pot. Add 2 cups of the bean water, bring to a boil over high heat, decrease the heat to medium, and simmer for 45 minutes or until the beans are tender, adding more of the bean water while cooking to assure that the beans are covered. When done, either mash until smooth or serve whole. Season to taste with salt.

To serve, cut the chicken into serving-sized pieces and arrange on a platter. Serve with the hot beans, hot steamed corn tortillas, and the salsa on the side. Guests can assemble their own grilled chicken tacos by pulling the chicken off the bone and placing it in the tortilla, then topping it with the salsa.

 # Tikka Chicken and Cauliflower Kebabs

SERVES: 4

HEAT SCALE: Mild

Thanks to Pat Chapman, England's King of Curries, for this recipe from one of his best-selling curry cookbooks. Tikka refers to food cut into small pieces and marinated. In this case the marinade is the same as the one used for the high-heat tandoori cooking, so it works very well with grilled foods. The green masala paste is available in Asian markets. These low-fat kebabs are usually served over rice with a spicy cucumber and yogurt salad on the side. Or serve as Pat does on a bed of shredded radicchio, white cabbage, and strips of red and green bell peppers, along with a chutney, either purchased or one of ours.

Green Tandoori Marinade
¼ cup plain yogurt
1 tablespoon vegetable oil
1 tablespoon freshly squeezed lemon
   juice
2 cloves garlic, chopped
3 green New Mexican chiles, roasted,
   peeled, stemmed, seeded, and
   chopped
1½ tablespoons chopped fresh mint
1½ tablespoons chopped fresh
   cilantro

1½ tablespoons green masala paste
½ teaspoon cumin seeds, toasted and
   ground
Pinch of salt
2 tablespoons milk, more or less

2 boneless, skinless chicken breasts,
   cut into 1½-inch cubes
1 small head cauliflower, cut into
   florets
2 cups cooked white rice
Chopped fresh parsley, for garnish

To make the marinade, place the yogurt, oil, lemon juice, garlic, chiles, mint, cilantro, and masala paste in a blender or food processor and purée to a smooth paste. Add the cumin seeds and a pinch of salt and pulse. While the machine is running, add just enough milk to form a purée that is easy to pour.

Toss the chicken in the marinade and cover. Marinate in the refrigerator for 24 hours.

Cook the cauliflower in a pot of boiling salted water until just tender, about 2 minutes, then drain. Rinse under cold water to stop the cooking. Toss in the marinade with the chicken to coat the cauliflower.

Thread the chicken and cauliflower on skewers, and grill over a medium fire for 10 to 14 minutes, turning occasionally. Cut open a sample of the chicken to check for doneness.

To serve, mound the rice on a serving platter, remove the chicken and cauliflower from the skewers and place them on the rice. Garnish with the parsley and serve.

Double-Spiced Barbecued Pineapple Chicken

SERVES: 4
HEAT SCALE: Hot

This method can be used for whole chicken or pieces such as legs and thighs. By spreading the paste under the skin, the juices from both the skin and the meat infuse the flavor of the paste into the chicken—and the evil, fatty, crispy, heavenly tasting skin.

Pineapple Paste
¼ cup chopped fresh cilantro
½ (5-ounce) can pineapple chunks, juice reserved
1 tablespoon freshly squeezed lime juice
1 tablespoon chopped red onion
½ habanero chile, stemmed, seeded, and minced, or ¼ teaspoon ground habanero chile
¼ teaspoon peeled and grated fresh ginger

4 chicken legs and thighs

Pineapple Barbecue Sauce
2 tablespoons chopped red onion
2 teaspoons olive oil
½ (5-ounce) can pineapple chunks, juice reserved
2 tablespoons ketchup
1 tablespoon freshly squeezed lime juice
1 tablespoon cider vinegar
1 tablespoon brown sugar
1 teaspoon soy sauce
½ to 1 habanero chile, stemmed and seeded
¼ cup fresh cilantro leaves

To make the paste, place all the ingredients in a blender or food processor and purée until smooth.

To prepare the chicken, "run" your finger between the skin and meat to loosen and make a pocket. Be sure to leave some of the skin attached. Gently stuff the paste into the pockets and pull the skin back over the chicken pieces. Set aside while you make the sauce.

To make the sauce, heat the oil in a saucepan over medium heat, and sauté the onion until softened. Reserving the cilantro, add all the remaining ingredients along with the reserved pineapple juice from the paste and sauce, about 6 tablespoons. Bring to a boil over high heat. Decrease the heat to medium-low and simmer for 30 minutes. Remove from the heat and transfer the sauce and the cilantro to a blender or food processor and purée until smooth. Keep the sauce warm while cooking the chicken.

Place the chicken on the grill, skin side up, and grill for 20 to 30 minutes over medium heat. Liberally baste the chicken with the sauce. Continue to cook until the chicken is done to an internal temperature of 160°.

To serve, place the chicken on a platter and brush with the sauce. Serve any remaining barbecue sauce on the side.

Caribbean Smoked Chicken with Habanero Marinade

SERVES: 4 to 6
HEAT SCALE: Medium

This is an ideal way to prepare chicken because it doesn't need to be turned and the fat and the marinade baste the bird as it smokes. Smoke with a delicate wood like apple so you don't mask the taste of the chicken. Serve with sliced avocados, rice, Curried Pineapple Serrano Salsa (p. 135), and warm banana bread.

Habanero Marinade
½ cup freshly squeezed orange juice
⅓ cup rum
½ cup chopped red onion
½ cup chopped green onion, green and white parts
2 habanero chiles, stemmed, seeded, and chopped
2 large cloves garlic, chopped

2 shallots, chopped
1 tablespoon chopped fresh thyme, or 1 teaspoon dried thyme
2 bay leaves, stemmed and crumbled
1 teaspoon salt
Freshly ground black pepper

⅓ cup vegetable oil
1 (3½- to 4-pound) chicken

To make the marinade, combine all the ingredients in a blender or food processor and purée until smooth. With the machine running, slowly pour in the oil until the mixture thickens.

Place the chicken in a deep nonreactive bowl. Loosen the skin on the chicken and rub the marinade under the skin. Fill the cavities with the marinade, rubbing it into the flesh. Pour the remaining marinade over the chicken and marinate, covered, in the refrigerator for 24 hours. Remove the chicken from the marinade and reserve the marinade.

Place the chicken on a rack in the smoker and smoke at 200° for 4 hours, basting occasionally with the marinade. Smoke for 4 hours (internal temperature at least 160°), then remove the chicken from the smoker and let it sit for 20 minutes before carving. Simmer any remaining marinade in a saucepan over medium-low heat for 20 minutes.

To serve, cut the chicken into serving pieces, arrange on a platter and top with the remaining marinade.

St. Kitts Jerk Chicken

SERVES: 4 to 6
HEAT SCALE: Hot

Nearly every island in the Caribbean has its version of this Jamaican specialty. This recipe is from our friends Neil and Sandy Mann, who perfected it when they were in the Peace Corps on the island. The marinade can also be used with pork. Serve this chicken with Habanero-Spiced Black Beans (p. 80), rice, and grilled tropical fruits such as pineapple, mangoes, and plantains (see sidebar p. 170).

Believe me, once you've had fresh smoked turkey, you'll wonder what the dry thing you used to eat for Thanksgiving really was.

—Richard Langer, *Where There's Smoke, There's Flavor*

Chicken, which is plain-tasting otherwise, benefits from marinating, especially skinless, boneless breasts.

—A. Cort Sinnes, *Gas Grill Gourmet.*

Jerk Marinade

2 bunches green onions, chopped,
white parts and some of the
greens
2 habanero chiles, stemmed, seeded
and minced
2 tablespoons soy sauce
2 tablespoons freshly squeezed lime
juice
5 teaspoons ground allspice

2 teaspoons dry mustard
2 bay leaves, stemmed and crumbled
2 cloves garlic, chopped
1½ teaspoons dried thyme,
crumbled
1 teaspoon straw or raw sugar
1 teaspoon ground cinnamon

4 to 6 skinless, boneless chicken
breasts

To make the marinade, combine all the ingredients in a blender or food processor and purée until smooth.

Pierce the chicken pieces with a fork so that the marinade will penetrate the meat. Put the chicken in a sealable plastic bag along with the marinade. Marinate in the refrigerator for at least 24 hours and up to 2 days.

Grill the chicken over a medium-hot fire for 10 minutes, turning occasionally until the chicken is done to an internal temperature of 160°.

Arrange the chicken on a platter and serve.

 # Mexican Chicken, Barbacoa-Style

SERVES: 4
HEAT SCALE: Medium

The word "barbecue" probably comes from the Spanish barbacoa, *but the two words no longer mean the same thing because* barbacoa *is cooked in a rock-lined pit. It is difficult to duplicate the flavor of wrapping meat or poultry in banana leaves and cooking it in a pit, but we're going to make a noble effort by grilling the chicken while it's covered with a chile paste. Serve with Chile-Grilled Potato Wedges (p. 68), grilled zucchini and corn, and warm corn or flour tortillas.*

Sesame-Chile Paste

8 guajillo chiles, or dried red New
Mexican chiles, stemmed and
seeded
4 chiles de árbol, stemmed and
seeded
2 tablespoons sesame seeds
1-inch piece cinnamon stick,
or 1 teaspoon ground cinnamon
8 whole allspice berries
6 whole cloves

2 teaspoons dried Mexican or other
oregano
½ cup chopped onion
4 cloves garlic, chopped
2 tablespoons cider vinegar
1 cup chicken broth
1 tablespoon vegetable oil

1 (3-pound) chicken, cut into serving
sized pieces
12 to 15 corn or flour tortillas

To make the paste, toast all the chiles on a hot dry griddle or skillet over medium-high heat until they turn slightly dark, taking care that they don't burn. Place in a bowl and cover with very hot water. Let them steep for 20 minutes until softened. Drain the chiles.

Toast the sesame seeds on the hot skillet until browned, taking care that they don't burn. Allow to cool.

Place the sesame seeds, cinnamon stick, allspice, and cloves in a spice grinder or coffee mill and process to a fine powder. Put the ground spices, chiles, oregano, onion, garlic, vinegar, and broth in a blender or food processor and purée until smooth. Strain if desired.

Heat the oil in a frying pan, add the sesame-chile purée, and sauté over medium heat, stirring occasionally, for 5 minutes to thicken. Allow to cool.

Spread the paste all over the chicken pieces (even under the skin), place in a sealable plastic bag, and refrigerate overnight.

Before grilling, be sure the pieces are thickly coated with the paste. Grill slowly, over a medium or low fire so the paste doesn't burn. Cook about 40 minutes, turning occasionally, or until the internal temperature reaches 160°.

Place the chicken on individual plates and serve with warmed tortillas on the side.

Bombay Grilled Chicken

SERVES: 4
HEAT SCALE: Medium

This recipe has a long list of ingredients, but it is easy to prepare and produces a complex flavor. Another plus, for health-conscious people, is that it is low in fat. As is typical of many Indian dishes, a spice paste is used first and then a marinade. The spiced yogurt marinade keeps the chicken moist even when grilling without the skin. Serve the chicken as they do in India on a bed of salat—*slivers of onion, with tomato wedges, radishes, and green chile garnished with lemon wedges and accompanied with curried potatoes and peas, and Coconut Mint Chutney (p. 146).*

Cayenne-Lemon Paste
3 tablespoons freshly squeezed
 lemon juice
2 tablespoons vegetable oil
2 teaspoons ground cayenne chile
1 teaspoon salt
½ teaspoon freshly ground black
 pepper

4 to 6 skinless, boneless chicken
 breasts

Curried Marinade
1½ cups plain yogurt
½ cup minced onion
3 tablespoons freshly squeezed
 lemon juice

2 tablespoons peanut or other
 vegetable oil
2 tablespoons peeled and minced
 fresh ginger
2 teaspoons ground cayenne chile
1 teaspoon ground cumin
1 teaspoon ground turmeric
1 teaspoon ground coriander
½ teaspoon ground cardamom
½ teaspoon ground cinnamon
¼ teaspoon ground nutmeg
⅛ teaspoon ground allspice
Freshly ground black pepper

Lemon wedges, for garnish
Chopped lettuce, for garnish

To make the paste, combine all the ingredients. Allow to sit at room temperature for 30 minutes to blend the flavors.

Make slits in the chicken pieces and rub the paste all over, making sure the paste gets in the slits. Let the chicken sit at room temperature for 30 minutes.

To make the marinade, place all the ingredients in a food processor or blender and process until smooth. Place the chicken in a nonreactive bowl and cover with the marinade. Marinate, in the refrigerator, covered, for 4 hours or overnight.

Remove the chicken from the marinade, reserving the marinade, and place on the grill over a medium-hot fire. Cover the grill and grill for 5 minutes. Turn the pieces, cover, and cook for an additional 5 minutes.

Uncover, turn the pieces, and baste with any remaining marinade. Continue cooking, uncovered, until the chicken is done, about 15 minutes or until the internal temperature is 160°.

To serve, arrange a bed of lettuce on a serving platter, place the chicken on top, and garnish with the lemon wedges.

Berber Chicken Stuffed with Fruited Rice

SERVES:　　　4 to 6

HEAT SCALE:　Mild

Here is a delicious chicken for special occasions. It is based on a recipe from the Berbers, a formerly nomadic people of Morocco. It has the flavor of the famous tajines but is cooked on a spit rather than as a stew. The ubiquitous mint appears in the marinade and as a garnish, and you can serve mint tea with this dish as well. For more flavor, rub the marinade under the skin of the chicken too. Just about any dried fruits will work in the rice, including peaches, cherries, and pears. Serve with North African Grilled Eggplant Salad (p. 169) and "Berber whiskey," which is mint tea.

Mint Marinade

2 tablespoons Moroccan Harissa
(p. 87) or ground red New
Mexican chile
¼ cup vegetable oil
¼ cup freshly squeezed lemon juice
2 teaspoons ground ginger
1 teaspoon ground cayenne chile
½ teaspoon ground turmeric
¼ teaspoon ground cumin
¼ cup finely chopped fresh mint, or
2 tablespoons dried mint
¼ cup water

1 (3- to 4-pound) chicken
Chopped fresh mint, for garnish
Sliced toasted almonds, for garnish

Fruited Rice

6 dried apricots
4 dried prunes
1 heaping teaspoon golden raisins
1 tablespoon olive oil
¼ cup chopped onions
2 cups cooked white rice
¼ cup blanched almonds
2 tablespoons chopped fresh mint
1 tablespoon Moroccan Harissa
(p. 87), or ½ to 1 teaspoon
ground cayenne chile
1 teaspoon ground ginger
1 teaspoon ground coriander
½ teaspoon ground cinnamon
¼ teaspoon ground turmeric
2 pinches pulverized saffron

To make the marinade, combine all the ingredients in a bowl and mix well.

Place the chicken in a plastic bag, add the marinade and marinate for 4 hours or overnight in the refrigerator. Remove the chicken from the marinade. Add a little water to the remaining marinade if needed to make it the right consistency for a basting sauce.

To make the rice, in a bowl cover the apricots, prunes, and raisins with hot water and soak for 15 to 20 minutes, until plump. Remove the fruit from the water and chop it into large pieces.

Heat the oil in a saucepan over medium heat, and sauté the onions until soft. In a bowl, combine all the remaining ingredients, mix well, and loosely stuff in the chicken. Any rice that doesn't fit inside the chicken can be reheated and served with the bird. Seal the opening with string or toothpicks and place the chicken on a spit.

Place the chicken on a rotisserie above a medium fire and cook, uncovered, for about 1½ hours, until done, or the internal temperature is 160°. While it is cooking, continue to baste with the marinade. If cooking with a covered grill, it will only take about 1 hour.

To serve, remove the rice from the chicken cavity and cut the chicken into serving pieces. Place the chicken on a platter, mound the rice in the center and garnish with the mint and almonds.

Tea-Smoked Sichuan Chicken

SERVES: 4

HEAT SCALE: Hot

This is a much easier version of the famous smoked duck, which involves marinating, steaming, drying, and smoking. You can even make this in a stove-top smoker. Any loose tea will work, even the orange pekoe used in most tea bags. The tea gives the skin an appealing color. If using chicken pieces, cut the marinade recipe in half. Serve with traditional Chinese foods such as spring rolls, white rice, and stir-fried vegetables.

Peppercorn Marinade
¼ cup Sichuan peppercorns
10 green onions, chopped, white and
  green parts
½ cup peanut oil
¼ cup peeled and chopped fresh
  ginger
⅓ cup rice wine or cooking sherry
2 tablespoons sugar
2 tablespoons grated orange zest
2 tablespoons crushed piquín chile,
  or other hot red chile
2 teaspoons sesame oil

Tea-Smoke Mixture
1 cup raw rice
⅔ cup firmly packed brown sugar
½ cup dry tea leaves
½ cup Sichuan peppercorns
14 whole star anise, broken into
  pieces
12 whole cloves
4 (2-inch) sticks cinnamon

Cayenne Finishing Oil
3 tablespoons sesame oil
2 teaspoons ground cayenne chile

1 (3½- to 4-pound) chicken or 4 legs
  and 4 thighs

To make the marinade, toast the Sichuan peppercorns on a dry skillet over medium heat until aromatic, taking care not to burn them. Crush them with a mortar and pestle. Combine with all the other ingredients for the marinade.

If you are using a whole chicken, tie the legs together. Place in a nonreactive pan or large plastic bag, cover with the marinade, and marinate for 24 hours in the refrigerator.

To make the tea-smoke mixture, combine all the ingredients. If you are using legs and thighs, place in a pan lined with aluminum foil in the stove-top smoker (see chapter 1 for stove-top smoking). If using a whole chicken and a smoker or grill, wrap the tea-smoke mixture in aluminum foil and poke holes in it. Place the foil on the coals or near the gas jets set on low. Smoke the chicken in 200° smoke for 3 to 4 hours or to an internal temperature of 160°.

> Backyard cooks have heaped a lot of abuse on poor chickens. . . . The slow-smoking process, in contrast, preserves the succulence of chickens and other fowl, while adding new dimensions of flavor.
>
> —Cheryl and Bill Jamison,
> *Smoke & Spice*

Preheat the oven to 450°. To make the finishing oil, combine the ingredients and let sit while the chicken is smoking.

Remove the chicken from the smoker, brush with the finishing oil, and place in the oven for 5 minutes to crisp the skin.

To serve, cut the chicken into serving pieces and arrange on a platter. Serve immediately.

Tuscan Devil Chicken

SERVES: 4

HEAT SCALE: Medium

In Italian, this chicken is called pollo alla diavolo *because of the addition of crushed red peperoncini chiles, the same kind sprinkled on pizzas to liven them up. Traditionally the chickens are split before grilling, but you can use a rotisserie if you wish—it just takes longer to cook. Add rosemary branches to the fire for a very aromatic smoke. Make this a true inferno of a meal off the grill and serve the devil chicken with Grilled Panzanella Salad (p. 163) and Grilled Jalapeño Polenta (p. 160).*

1 (4-pound) chicken

Devil Marinade
⅔ cup dry red wine, such as Chianti
⅓ cup olive oil
2 tablespoons freshly squeezed
    lemon juice
1½ tablespoons finely chopped fresh
    rosemary, or 2 teaspoons dried
    rosemary

1½ tablespoons finely chopped fresh
    sage, or 2 teaspoons dried sage
2 teaspoons crushed red chile: piquín
    (hot) or ground New Mexican red
    chile (mild)
2 cloves garlic
¼ teaspoon salt

Chopped fresh rosemary, for garnish

To prepare the chicken, use poultry shears or a heavy knife to cut down
both sides of the backbone and cut the chicken in half. Remove the backbone and place the chicken on a cutting board skin side up. Press hard on
the breastbone to break it and flatten the bird.

To make the marinade, in a bowl, whisk together all the ingredients.
Coat the chicken with the marinade, place in a plastic bag, and marinate for
2 hours in the refrigerator.

Lightly oil a clean grill surface. Remove the chicken from the marinade
and reserve the marinade. Place chicken on the grill, skin side down, and
weigh it down with a cast-iron skillet so the chicken remains flat. Grill for
15 to 20 minutes per side, basting frequently with the marinade, until the
juices run clear when pierced with a fork, or when the internal temperature
reaches 160°.

Using a cleaver, chop the split chicken halves into quarters. Arrange the
quarters on a large platter. Garnish with the rosemary, and serve.

Greek Grilled Chicken

SERVES: 4
HEAT SCALE: Mild

Sure we added some nontraditional chiles to this recipe. The Greeks have been needing
them since 1500 B.C.E. but had to wait until now, more than 3,000 years later. This
marinade can also be used on lamb kebabs as an appetizer to a Greek feast. Retsina is

a wine flavored with pine resin—an acquired taste for sipping, but one that works very well in a marinade. Serve with a traditional Greek salad of tossed greens, kalamata olives, and feta cheese, along with Nutty Rice Pilaf (p. 85), and green beans.

Greek Marinade

⅓ cup freshly squeezed lemon juice

¼ cup *retsina* or dry white wine

2 tablespoons olive oil

1 tablespoon chopped fresh oregano, or 1 teaspoon dried oregano

1 teaspoon ground cinnamon

2 teaspoons chopped fresh thyme, or ¾ teaspoon dried thyme

2 jalapeño chiles, stemmed, seeded, and chopped

Salt and freshly ground black pepper

---

4 boneless, skinless chicken breasts

To make the marinade, place all the ingredients in a blender or food processor and purée until smooth. Place the chicken breasts in a plastic bag, coat with the marinade, and marinate for 2 hours in the refrigerator.

Remove the chicken from the marinade and place the marinade in a small saucepan. Simmer the marinade for 20 minutes over medium heat. Grill the breasts over a medium fire, basting with the marinade, for about 20 minutes or until the internal temperature reaches 160°.

Place the chicken breasts on individual dishes and serve at once.

Smoked Mexican Turkey with Orange–Chile Oil Marinade

SERVES: 4 to 6

HEAT SCALE: Mild

Here's a double Mexican influence—turkeys as well as chiles are native to the Americas. This recipe will work with a breast as well as the legs. If using a whole turkey or breast, increase the amount of the marinade and inject the marinade into the bird as well as basting it while it's smoking. Use any Mexican chiles such as ancho, pasilla, cascabel, or guajillo. Anchiote paste is available in Hispanic markets. Serve with avocado slices, Frijoles Borrachos (p. 109), and grilled corn on the cob or Grilled Corn with African Nitir Kebe (p. 159), along with corn tortillas.

Orange–Chile Oil Marinade

½ cup vegetable oil
6 cascabel chiles, stemmed and
 seeded
¼ cup chopped onion
2 cloves garlic, minced
1 teaspoon cumin seeds
2 teaspoons achiote paste
1 cup freshly squeezed orange juice

1 tablespoon freshly squeezed lime
 juice
1 teaspoon dried Mexican or domestic oregano
Pinch of ground cloves
Salt and freshly ground black pepper

_____

4 turkey legs

Heat the oil in a pan over medium heat, add the chiles and onion, and sauté until softened. Add the garlic and cumin and continue to sauté for an additional minute. Remove the pan from the heat.

Combine the oil mixture with all the other marinade ingredients in a food processor or blender and purée until smooth.

Make slits in the turkey to allow the marinade to penetrate. Place the turkey and marinade in a large plastic bag and marinate overnight in the refrigerator.

Prepare the smoker using hickory or pecan wood and smoke the legs in 200° smoke for 3 to 3½ hours or until the turkey is done to an internal temperature of 160°. If you wish to continue marinating, simmer the marinade in a pan over medium-low heat for 20 minutes and brush it over the legs occasionally. When done, remove the turkey from the smoker and brush one final time with the marinade.

To serve, slice the smoked turkey off the legs, arrange on a platter, and top with any remaining marinade.

It's a Man Thang

It's the caveman in us. I think that's why you see more and more men barbecuing. It's a macho thing. Playing with fire and being outdoors, bragging about how good you cook, it's got all the macho rush to it without any of the violence. Also women do not pursue it very thoroughly. That's one territory they don't try to invade. They kind of leave it to us.

—Jim "Arkansas Trav'ler" Quessenberry

Mesquite-Grilled Turkey Legs with Jalapeño-Cilantro-Lime Basting Sauce

SERVES: 4
HEAT SCALE: Medium

This is one of the simpler and quicker ways to prepare turkey. You can add mesquite chips soaked in water to the fire to add a little smoke flavor. And go ahead, be daring, add a couple of tablespoons of tequila to the sauce. Serve with potato salad, ranch-style baked beans, and Chile and Dried Cherry Chocolate Dessert (p. 170).

Basting Sauce
¾ cup chopped fresh cilantro
¼ cup freshly squeezed lime juice
6 jalapeño chiles, stemmed, seeded, and chopped
2 fresh tomatillos
2 cloves garlic, chopped
2 tablespoons vegetable oil

1½ teaspoon sugar
½ teaspoon ground coriander
¼ teaspoon freshly ground white pepper

4 small turkey legs
Chopped fresh cilantro, for garnish

To make the basting sauce, place all the ingredients in a blender or food processor and purée, adding some water, if necessary for a smooth consistency.

Bring the turkey to room temperature and gently loosen the skin without tearing. Brush the sauce over the legs and under the skin, and reserve any remaining sauce. Allow the turkey to sit at room temperature for 1 hour.

Grill the turkey legs over a medium fire, basting regularly with the sauce. Cook for 30 minutes, turning often, or until the internal temperature of the legs reaches 160° for medium.

Arrange the turkey legs on a platter, garnish with the cilantro, and serve.

Pasilla-Tamarind Barbecued Ostrich

SERVES: 4
HEAT SCALE: Mild

We debated for weeks whether to include ostrich as meat or as poultry. Finally we decided it was a really big bird and belongs in the poultry chapter, even though it tastes like meat, not chicken. You can use tamarind pods in this recipe, but buying the paste in an Asian market is so much easier. Tamarind is popular in both Mexican and Asian recipes, and the pasilla chiles work well with it because of their raisin-like flavor. The sweet heat of the sauce goes well with a simple baked potato with chives and broccoli spears.

Basting Sauce
4 pasilla chiles, stemmed and seeded
½ cup tamarind paste
1½ cups water
¼ cup firmly packed brown sugar
1 tablespoon tomato sauce

2 cloves garlic, minced
2 tablespoons freshly squeezed lime
   juice

4 ostrich steaks about 1 inch thick
Chopped fresh parsley, for garnish

Place the chiles in a bowl and cover with hot water. Let them steep for 20 minutes to soften, then drain.

In a medium-sized saucepan, combine the tamarind paste and water and warm over medium heat, until the paste is dissolved. Press the mixture through a sieve to strain out the fibers and seeds.

Place all the basting sauce ingredients, including the softened chiles, in a blender or food processor and purée until smooth.

Grill the ostrich steaks over a medium-hot fire, basting frequently with the sauce, for about 7 minutes each side or until the internal temperature reaches 150° for medium-rare. Simmer the basting sauce for 20 minutes in a saucepan over medium-low heat.

To serve, place the ostrich on individual plates, top with the basting sauce, and garnish with the parsley.

Sweet and Hot Gingered Plum Smoked Duck

SERVES: 4
HEAT SCALE: Medium

For some unknown reason, smoked poultry benefits from a marinade that is somewhat sweet. The duck can also be grilled over indirect heat, if you don't want such a smoky flavor. Use a fruitwood such as apple or apricot for the smoking. Simple white rice is a nice accompaniment to this elegant dish.

Plum and Ginger-Chile Sauce

1 (16-ounce) can purple plums, pitted and drained, reserve the syrup

2 tablespoons peeled and grated fresh ginger

2 cloves garlic, chopped

2 tablespoons crushed chiltepíns, or other hot red chile

2 tablespoons brown sugar or honey

2 tablespoons dry sherry

1 tablespoon hoisin sauce

1 tablespoon soy sauce

1 tablespoon Asian plum sauce

4 star anise

2 tablespoons distilled white vinegar

1 (4- to 5-pound) duck

Salt and freshly ground black pepper

2 green onions, white and green parts

2 cloves garlic

2 (1-inch) pieces peeled fresh ginger

To make the sauce, put the plums, ginger, and garlic in a blender or food processor and purée until smooth, thinning with some of the reserved syrup if necessary to maintain consistency.

In a saucepan, combine all the ingredients for the sauce, including the syrup but excluding the vinegar, and simmer over low heat for 30 minutes to thicken. Add the vinegar and continue to simmer for 10 more minutes. Remove from the heat and discard the star anise.

Cover the duck inside and out and under the skin with the sauce. Place in a plastic bag and marinate in the refrigerator overnight. Remove the duck from the marinade, reserve the marinade, and allow the duck to come to room temperature before smoking. Season the cavity with salt and pepper and put the onions, garlic and ginger inside. Inject the duck with more marinade if desired.

Build a fire in the smoker and bring the smoke to 200 to 220°. Smoke the duck for 4 hours, basting occasionally with the marinade.

Heat the remaining marinade and simmer for 20 minutes over medium-low heat, thinning with a little water if it thickens while simmering.

Remove the duck from the smoker, brush with the sauce, and cut into serving pieces. Arrange on a platter and serve with the sauce on the side.

 # Habanero-Marinated and Pecan-Smoked Quail *(pictured in photo section)*

SERVES: 6
HEAT SCALE: Hot

The wild quail most commonly eaten are the bobwhite and the crested, or Gambel's quail of the west, that have white meat. The Courternix, a domesticated variety, is raised on farms in South Carolina and Georgia. The taste can be mild to strong depending on the age of the bird. Quail are small and lean, so they must be marinated before cooking. The lengthy marinating time is countered by the short time it takes to smoke these birds. Serve with Grilled Spring Asparagus with Spicy Lemon Mop (p. 167).

Marinade
¼ cup golden raisins
¼ cup soy sauce
2 habanero chiles, stemmed, seeded, and chopped
4 cloves garlic, chopped
2 tablespoons peeled and minced fresh ginger

2 teaspoons ground coriander
1 teaspoon ground turmeric
1 teaspoon ground cinnamon
½ teaspoon ground cloves
Juice of 2 limes
⅓ cup vegetable oil

6 whole quail

In a bowl, soak the raisins in the soy sauce for 15 minutes to soften. Place the raisins and the soy sauce and all the remaining marinade ingredients, except for the oil, in a blender or food processor and purée until smooth, adding the oil a little at a time with the motor running. Place the quail in a non-reactive pan or in a large plastic bag and marinate in the refrigerator for 24 hours, or overnight if you are strapped for time.

Delicate in texture but big in flavor, quail is perfect for grilling.
—Janet Hazen,
New Game Cuisine

Build a fire with pecan or fruitwood and bring the smoke to 200 to 220°. Place the quail on a rack in the smoker and smoke until the leg bones move easily, about 1½ hours. Or smoke-grill the quail over a hot fire for 20 to 25 minutes, turning often, until the leg bones move easily. In either case, the internal temperature should be 160°.

To serve, arrange the quail on a large platter.

EIGHT

Spiced-up Seafood
Infused with Flames and Smoke

IF YOU THINK CHICKEN is difficult to cook on the grill, try grilling fish. At least chicken breasts don't fall apart and crumble into the fire. But fish can and does, especially if it sticks to the grill and you try turning it with a spatula. Another possible disaster is a tendency for fatty fish, or fish saturated with oils in the marinade, to burn intensely during a flare-up. Dave lost a mackerel fillet that way on a charcoal grill on the beach in Islamorada, Florida. "The fatty fish ignited like a flare and before I could run for water, the fillet resembled a stick of charcoal," he notes for the record. Even a minor flare-up that catches the fish on fire can spoil its flavor, so have a squirt gun or spray bottle nearby whenever you grill fish or other seafood.

Another thing that can go wrong with grilled fish is the dreaded over-marination. Fish has this tendency to absorb the marinade so much that the intense flavors can overwhelm the fish, especially delicate whitefish. Stick to the suggested marinade times in the individual recipes.

It is especially important to have a clean, well-oiled grill surface when working with fish, and a fish grill basket as described in chapter 1 is not only recommended for the fillets in this chapter, but is also handy for the steaks. You can also buy special fish turners. They have tongs like a fork that fit into the spaces in the grill so that you can get under the piece of fish without scraping.

Smoking fish is less confrontational. A light smoke can be applied during the grilling process, but the most intense smoke is usually reserved for thick hunks of salmon that have been treated with a liquid spice cure first.

Fish on the Grill Preparation Hints

Fish and seafood pick up marinade flavors quickly. Marinating for 15 minutes to an hour should be sufficient. Do not over-marinate, or fish flesh will break down and become mushy. At their simplest, marinades and bastes can be a light application of oil with salt and pepper seasoning. Woods and herbs added to the gill offer another means of flavor enhancement. Fish cooks so quickly over a hot fire that your addition of soaked wood chips or herbs will not penetrate as effectively as will slow smoking with a closed-lid grill. But, the heavenly odor in your backyard is worth a try.

—Karen Adler, *Hooked on Fish on the Grill*

In chapter 7, we noted the lack of cook-offs devoted to barbecued chicken; interestingly enough, there are several devoted to salmon in California and Washington!

We mentioned in chapter 1 that it is very difficult to take the temperature of fish with an instant-read thermometer, which necessitates "eyeballing" the fish to see when it is done. The rule of thumb for seafood is that fish is done when the outside flakes easily with a fork, and shrimp and scallops are done when they lose their translucency and become opaque.

Belizean Rubbed and Grilled Fish Burger

SERVES: 4

HEAT SCALE: Medium

This particular "burger" is a fired-up re-creation of a fish sandwich Nancy devoured in the tiny town of San Pedro on Ambergris Caye, Belize in 1985. The restaurant was called Elvie's Burger Isle, and the diners sat outside under a tamarind tree on picnic benches. If ever there was a simple-to-prepare, quick-and-easy fish recipe with significant heat, this is it. Serve with french fries, crisp coleslaw, and to toast Elvie, a frosty tamarind soda.

1 teaspoon ground habanero chile
1 teaspoon garlic salt
1 teaspoon ground thyme
½ teaspoon ground allspice
¼ teaspoon ground nutmeg
4 small whitefish fillets, such as
   snapper, trigger fish, or grouper
Olive oil
4 rolls

Possible Sauces to Serve over the Fish
Smoked Fruit Salsa (p. 43)
Puerto Rican Mojo Sauce (p. 78)
Curried Pineapple Serrano Salsa
   (p. 135)
Serrano Cilantro Aioli (p. 164)

In a bowl, combine the chile, garlic salt, thyme, allspice, and nutmeg. Brush the fillets with olive oil and dust with the spice mixture. Allow to sit at room temperature while you prepare the grill.

Cut the rolls in half lengthwise and brush with oil.

Grill the fish in a grill basket over medium heat until done, about 5 minutes per side, or until the fillets flake.

Grill the rolls to slightly toasted. To serve, place the fish on the rolls and top with a sauce of choice, even if it's not in this book or is store-bought.

Chile-Infused Red Snapper, Veracruz-Style

SERVES: 4 to 6
HEAT SCALE: Mild

This is one of the most delicious Mexican coastal fish recipes. It is served in Veracruz, the area of Mexico most influenced by Spanish cooking, but is popular all over the country. Often the snapper is dusted with flour and pan fried, then covered with a sauce, but we prefer ours beach-style. We grill it over wood or natural charcoal (gas is acceptable, too) and then serve it with the sauce on the side. Charring the tomatoes on the grill adds a smoky dimension to the sauce. This elegant and colorful fish is served with white rice, additional pickled jalapeños and an equally elegant dessert such as Grilled Rum Bananas with Nutmeg Whipped Cream (p. 172).

1 (3- to 4-pound) whole dressed red snapper
Juice of 1 lime
¼ cup ground chile de árbol or red New Mexican chile
1 teaspoon salt
Olive oil
2 to 3 cups cooked white rice

Chopped fresh parsley, for garnish
Sliced jalapeño chiles, for garnish

Veracruz Sauce
6 small tomatoes
1 small onion

1 tablespoon olive oil
3 cloves garlic
½ cup sliced pimiento-stuffed olives
1 tablespoon freshly squeezed lemon juice
2 bay leaves
4 canned pickled jalapeño chiles, seeded and cut into thin strips
1 tablespoon juice from the pickled jalapeños
1 tablespoon capers
½ teaspoon sugar
¼ teaspoon ground cinnamon
¼ teaspoon ground cloves
Salt and freshly ground pepper

With a knife, lightly score the fish on both sides. Sprinkle the lime juice over the whole fish, inside and out. In a small bowl, combine the chile and salt and mix well. Sprinkle the fish with the mixture, inside and out.

To make the sauce, roast the tomatoes and onion on the grill over a medium fire until charred evenly. Remove from the grill and chop. In a small pan, heat the oil over medium heat. Sauté the garlic in the oil until lightly browned. Add the tomatoes and onions and bring to a boil over high heat. Decrease the heat to low, add the remaining ingredients and simmer until thickened, about 15 minutes. Remove the bay leaves.

Place the fish on the grill indirectly over a medium fire, baste with olive oil, and cook for about 30 minutes, turning twice and basting with the oil. The fish should flake easily and the internal temperature at its thickest part should be 135° for medium.

Place the fish on a serving platter and spoon the rice around the fish. Pour most of the sauce over the fish and garnish with the parsley and some sliced jalapeño chiles. At the table, carve the fish and serve it on the rice with additional sauce poured over the top.

Grilled Salmon Steaks with Green Chile–Lime Sauce

SERVES: 4
HEAT SCALE: Medium

Here is a simple salmon recipe that's quick to prepare but tastes great. You can literally whip it up while you are starting the grill. Feel free to flavor this with a little light smoke—say apple or other fruitwoods. Serve with a chilled white wine.

4 salmon steaks
Olive oil
Salt and freshly ground black pepper

Green Chile–Lime Sauce
½ cup chopped fresh cilantro
2 cloves garlic, chopped

3 roasted and peeled New Mexico
    green chiles, stemmed and
    seeded
Juice of 1 lime
1 tablespoon vegetable oil
1 teaspoon grated lime zest

Brush the steaks with the oil and season with salt and pepper.

To make the sauce, place all the ingredients in a blender or food processor and purée until smooth.

Grill the steaks over a medium fire for about 8 minutes, turning several times, or until the fish flakes on the outside.

To serve, pour some of the sauce on individual plates, place the steaks on the sauce, and top with additional sauce.

Coconut-Smoked Mahi-Mahi with Curried Pineapple-Serrano Salsa

SERVES: 4
HEAT SCALE: Medium

Mahi-mahi is the Hawaiian term for the fish called dorado *in Spanish and* dolphin fish *in English. This recipe also works well with "fishier" fish such as kingfish, bluefish, and mackerel. Yes, you can substitute steaks for the fillets, but be sure to adjust the cooking time. Smoking with coconut gives the fish a sweet flavor with tropical overtones. This recipe is designed for a water smoker or a charcoal grill with indirect heat, a water-filled pan beneath the fish, and the coconut placed on the coals. Use a fish grill basket with handles for easy turning.*

¼ cup vegetable oil
2 tablespoons rice wine
Juice of 1 lime
2 teaspoons ground habanero chile
1 teaspoon peeled and minced fresh ginger
4 mahi-mahi fillets, or snapper or grouper
1 fresh coconut, broken into pieces, reserving the milk

Curried Pineapple-Serrano Salsa
1 ripe pineapple, peeled, cored, and cut into ¼-inch slices
3 serrano chiles, stemmed and chopped
2 tablespoons rice cooking wine
1 tablespoon freshly squeezed orange juice
2 teaspoons curry powder
2 teaspoons brown sugar
1 tablespoon chopped fresh cilantro

The Barbecue Bombast Simile

If barbecue were an argument, it'd be a beer brawl. Barbecue fanatics debate it, dissect it, discuss it, analyze it, judge it, go on expeditions in search of some of the best plates of it, celebrate it, scorn the pretenders of it, and finally, they eat it. And they do all of this with sanctimony, belligerence, or both.

—Jim Shahin, "Barbecue Capital of the World."

In a bowl, combine the oil, rice wine, lime juice, chile, and ginger to make a marinade. Place the fish in a nonreactive dish, pour the marinade over the top, and marinate, covered, at room temperature for 30 to 45 minutes.

Prepare a fire in a water smoker or a charcoal grill and when hot, place the coconut pieces on the coals. Pour the reserved coconut milk into the water pan of the smoker along with the water. Smoke the fish for 1 to 2 hours or until the fish flakes, keeping a very low heat. You may quickly baste a couple of times with the marinade, if desired, to keep the fish from drying out.

To make the salsa, grill the pineapple slices or heat in a pan over medium heat for 5 to 10 minutes, until browned. Dice the pineapple. Combine all the ingredients for the salsa, except for the cilantro, and allow to sit at room temperature for an hour to blend the flavors. Toss with the cilantro.

Place the fish on individual plates, top with a little salsa, and serve the remaining salsa on the side.

It's a Man Thang, Part 2

It was the popularity of outdoor barbecues that led most American husbands to take an interest in cookery. While the kitchen had come to be regarded as woman's sphere from frontier days onward, cooking out of doors was different. It reminded grown men of Boy Scout days when they roasted hot dogs over campfires. Building up the fire in the charcoal grill was thoroughly masculine. So was the cooking of a steak. Before long, the barbecue cooks were adding sauces to their outdoor masterpieces and, once caught by the spell of creative cooking, began to launch into intricate and unusual dishes.

—Betty Wason, *Cooks, Gluttons, and Gourmets*

Caribbean Wine-Grilled Grouper with Pineapple-Ginger Sauce

SERVES: 4
HEAT SCALE: Medium

Dave had his first taste of fresh grouper in Charlotte Amalie in the U.S. Virgin Islands in 1968 when he bought it at a market and was fortunate that the guest house where he was staying had a charcoal grill. When basted with what essentially is a highly spiced white wine butter sauce, this grouper achieves noble dimensions. Note that the basting sauce can be prepared ahead of time and reheated before use. This recipe can also be a base for a great luncheon salad. Place the steaks on a bed of baby mixed greens, julienned carrots, and thinly sliced green bell peppers, topped with the Pineapple-Ginger Sauce and toasted sliced almonds or macadamia nuts.

Habanero-Wine Basting Sauce

⅓ cup butter
½ cup pineapple juice
¼ cup dry white wine
1 habanero chile, stemmed, seeded, and minced
1 teaspoon chopped fresh cilantro
Freshly ground white pepper

2 tablespoons cornstarch
2 tablespoons peeled and minced fresh ginger
1 tablespoon minced habanero chile
2 teaspoons soy sauce
1 cup water
½ cup pineapple chunks
2 tablespoons dry white wine

Pineapple-Ginger Sauce

¼ cup pineapple juice
¼ cup freshly squeezed lime juice
¼ cup sugar

2 cups cooked white rice
4 grouper steaks, 1 inch thick, or swordfish
Chopped fresh cilantro, for garnish

To make the basting sauce, melt the butter over low heat in a small saucepan. Whisk in all the remaining ingredients and mix well.

To make the sauce, combine the pineapple juice, lime juice, sugar, and cornstarch in a saucepan and stir until smooth. Add the ginger, habanero, soy sauce, and water, and mix well. Simmer the sauce over medium heat, stirring constantly until it is transparent and thick. Stir in the pineapple chunks and wine.

Grill the fish over a medium fire, turning occasionally for about 8 minutes or until the fish flakes on the outside, basting frequently with the basting sauce.

To serve, place the fish on a bed of rice, top with the sauce, and garnish with the chopped cilantro.

VARIATION: Salmon or halibut fillets may be substituted.

 ## Wasabi-Marinated Ahi Tuna with Asian Chile Slaw

SERVES: 4
HEAT SCALE: Mild

Wasabi is an extremely powerful Japanese horseradish that can be found as a powder or as a paste in easy-to-use tubes. If using it as a powder, reconstitute it in rice wine vinegar. Thai fish sauce, or nam pla, is available in Asian markets. This tuna should be served medium-rare. The crisp, fresh taste of the coleslaw is a nice accompaniment to the spicy tuna.

Wasabi Marinade
5 tablespoons rice wine vinegar
2 tablespoons soy sauce
1½ tablespoons wasabi paste
1½ tablespoons peeled and grated
   fresh ginger
1 tablespoon vegetable oil

1 tablespoon minced shallot
1 tablespoon hot mustard
2 cloves garlic, minced
1 serrano or jalapeño chile,
   stemmed, seeded, and minced

4 ahi tuna steaks or swordfish

Asian Chile Dressing

⅓ cup peanut or vegetable oil

1 tablespoon cider vinegar

¼ cup rice wine vinegar

2 teaspoons Thai fish sauce (*nam pla*)

2 teaspoons sesame oil

2 teaspoons sugar

4 small fresh Thai chiles (*prik kee nu*) or 2 serrano chiles, stemmed and minced

2 teaspoons finely sliced green onions, white and green parts

Salt and white pepper

Asian Chile Slaw

2 cups finely shredded napa or regular cabbage

¼ cup shredded carrot

¼ cup finely sliced green onion, white and green parts

¼ cup sliced edible pea pods, sliced lengthwise

¼ cup chopped peanuts, for garnish

Chopped fresh cilantro, for garnish

To make the marinade, in a bowl, combine all the ingredients and allow to sit at room temperature for 20 minutes to blend the flavors.

Place the fish in a single layer in a nonreactive bowl, pour the marinade over the fish, and turn to coat. Cover and marinate for an hour at room temperature.

To make the slaw dressing, whisk together all the ingredients and allow to sit, covered, at room temperature for 30 minutes to blend the flavors.

Grill the fish over a medium fire for about 10 minutes, turning occasionally, until just done, for medium-rare. Cut one of the steaks open to check for doneness.

To make the salad, toss together the cabbage, carrot, onion, and pea pods. Toss with just enough of the dressing to coat. Garnish with the peanuts and cilantro.

To serve, place the fish on individual plates and serve with a scoop of the slaw.

Grilled Tuna with Ras El Hanout Spice Rub and Yogurt-Cilantro Sauce

SERVES: 4
HEAT SCALE: Medium

The key to the unique flavor of this recipe is the versatile Moroccan spice rub that can also be used with grilled chicken and lamb. Ras el hanout literally means "top of the shop," and is a mixture of many spices. Some extreme recipes are reputed to have about one hundred ingredients. In addition to seasoning meats, it also spices up rice and couscous. Our Jalapeño-Cilantro Couscous (p. 149) goes well with this dish.

Ras El Hanout Spice Rub
1 teaspoon cumin seeds
1 teaspoon caraway seeds
¼ teaspoon cardamom seeds
1 (2-inch) stick cinnamon
6 allspice berries
4 whole cloves
½ cup chopped onion
2 teaspoons peeled and grated fresh
    ginger
1½ teaspoons freshly ground black
    pepper
1 teaspoon ground cayenne chile

1 teaspoon ground coriander
¼ teaspoon ground nutmeg
¼ teaspoon ground turmeric
2 tablespoons vegetable oil

4 tuna steaks, 1 inch thick

Yogurt-Cilantro Sauce
½ cup plain yogurt
2 tablespoons finely chopped fresh
    cilantro
1 clove garlic, minced
2 teaspoons grated lemon zest

To make the spice rub, place the cumin, caraway, and cardamom seeds in a hot, dry skillet over medium-low heat and toast until the seeds start to pop and are very fragrant. Remove the skillet from the heat and allow the seeds to cool in the skillet. Place in a spice grinder along with the cinnamon, allspice, and cloves and process to a fine powder. Sift if you want a finer spice rub.

Transfer the spices to a blender or food processor and add the onion, ginger, black pepper, cayenne, coriander, nutmeg, and turmeric along with the oil. Process into a paste, adding a little water if more liquid is needed to form a paste.

Rub the paste on the fish and marinate in a bowl, covered, at room temperature, for an hour.

To make the sauce, combine all the ingredients in a bowl and allow to sit at room temperature to blend the flavors.

Grill the fish over a medium-low heat, being careful the paste doesn't burn, for 8 to 10 minutes, until it flakes on the outside.

To serve, spread some of the sauce on individual plates and place the fish on top of it. Swizzle the remaining sauce artistically over the grilled steaks and serve.

 # Bayou-Grilled Catfish with Creole Mustard Sauce

SERVES: 4

HEAT SCALE: Mild

Creole and Cajun cuisines are not considered to be bastions of barbecue and grilling, but the people in Louisiana certainly know how to cook fish. If you are counting calories, you can get rid of a few by substituting a plain, low-fat yogurt for the sour cream. The sauce also goes well with other seafood dishes and replaces a red tomato–based sauce. You better put the leftover hot sauce on the table, too.

You Know Where to Put Those Lower Ranks, You Limey!

The people are extremely fond of an entertainment which they call a barbecue. It consists of a large party of people meeting together to partake of a sturgeon or pig roasted while in the open air, on a sort of low hurdle, over a slow fire; this, however, is an entertainment confined chiefly to the lower ranks.

—Englishman Jonathan Weld on his visit to the United States, 1799

The Hot Sauce Marinade

3 teaspoons olive oil

2 cloves garlic, crushed

2 teaspoons freshly cracked black
  pepper

2 teaspoons Louisiana-style hot
  sauce

1 teaspoon distilled white vinegar

—————————————

4 catfish fillets

Creole Mustard Sauce

½ cup heavy cream

3 tablespoons sour cream or yogurt

3 tablespoons Creole mustard or
  other coarse-grained mustard

2 teaspoons Worcestershire sauce

2 teaspoons prepared horseradish

1 teaspoon prepared yellow mustard

1 teaspoon Louisiana-style hot sauce

1 teaspoon honey

¼ teaspoon salt

¼ teaspoon freshly ground white
  pepper

½ teaspoon dried basil

To make the marinade, combine all the ingredients in a bowl, stir well, and allow to sit for 20 minutes to blend the flavors.

Place the fillets in a pan, spread them with the marinade, and let sit at room temperature, covered, for 1 hour.

To make the sauce, combine all the ingredients in a saucepan over medium heat and simmer for 10 minutes. Remove the pan from the heat and allow to cool to room temperature.

Place the fillets in a grill basket with handles and grill over a medium fire, turning occasionally, until the fish flakes easily, about 6 minutes.

To serve, place the fillets on individual plates and pour 1 tablespoon of the sauce over each, with the extra sauce served on the side.

 # Sichuan-Marinated Grilled Tilapia Fillets with Three-Chile Sweet and Sour Sauce

SERVES: 4

HEAT SCALE: Hot

Tilapia, a farm-raised fish originally from Asia, is mild and sweet-tasting with a deli-cate flesh. You can substitute catfish or flounder fillets if you can't find tilapia. These are the fish most enjoyed by people who don't like "fishy" fish. They work particularly well for our chile-infused recipes because they are soft and absorb the marinade quickly. Use a fish grill basket (see chapter 1) for ease in turning the fillets without destroying them. Sichuan peppercorns, Asian plum sauce, and Asian chilli garlic paste are available at Asian markets.

Sichuan Marinade

1 teaspoon Sichuan peppercorns
¼ cup dry sherry
1 tablespoon peeled and finely chopped fresh ginger
1 green onion, finely chopped, white and green parts
1 teaspoon minced garlic
1 teaspoon sesame oil
½ teaspoon crushed santaka chile or other small, hot red chile

4 tilapia fillets
Minced green onion, white and green parts, for garnish

Three-Chile Sweet and Sour Sauce

¾ cup chicken broth
¼ cup rice wine vinegar
2 tablespoons Asian plum sauce
1 tablespoon sugar
1 tablespoon cornstarch
½ teaspoon sesame oil
1 tablespoon peanut or vegetable oil
1 green onion, chopped, white and green parts
1 teaspoon peeled and minced fresh ginger
4 whole santaka chiles, piquín chiles, or other small hot, red chiles
2 tablespoons Asian chilli garlic paste
1 tablespoon ground red New Mexican chile

To make the marinade, toast the Sichuan peppercorns in a hot, unoiled frying pan over high heat until fragrant. Remove from the heat, let cool, and crush. Combine in a bowl with the other marinade ingredients, and allow to sit for 30 minutes to blend the flavors.

Place the fish in a nonreactive dish, pour the marinade over the fish, and marinate, covered, for an hour at room temperature.

To make the sauce, whisk together the broth, vinegar, plum sauce, sugar, cornstarch, and sesame oil in a bowl.

Heat a wok until hot and add the peanut oil. Add the onion, ginger, and santaka chiles and stir-fry for a couple of minutes. Add the chile paste and stir-fry for a minute. Add the broth mixture and the red chile powder and stir well. Increase to high heat and bring to a boil, then decrease the heat to medium and simmer until thickened, about 5 minutes. Remove the whole chiles.

Place the fillets in a grill basket with handles and grill over a medium fire until they flake with a fork, 8 to 10 minutes, turning occasionally. Take care that the fillets don't burn.

To serve, pour a little of the sauce on the plate, place the fish on top, and garnish with the green onion.

Marinated and Grilled Fish, Middle Eastern–Style

SERVES: 4
HEAT SCALE: Medium

Because there are more than a dozen countries that can be classified as Middle Eastern, this recipe reflects a style rather than a single country. It is designed so that the spice flavors don't overwhelm the fish. Again, use a fish grill basket with handles to protect the fillets. Our North African Grilled Eggplant Salad with Garlic-Cayenne Dressing (p. 169) makes a perfect accompaniment to this fish dish.

Marinade
½ cup chopped onion
2 jalapeño chiles, stemmed, seeded, and chopped
1 large clove garlic, chopped
2 tablespoons freshly squeezed lemon juice
1 tablespoon olive oil

½ teaspoon ground paprika
½ teaspoon ground cinnamon
¼ teaspoon ground cumin
Freshly ground black pepper

4 whitefish fillets such as snapper
Chopped fresh parsley, for garnish
Lemon wedges, for garnish

Place all the marinade ingredients in a blender or food processor and purée until smooth. Place the fillets in a glass dish and pour the marinade over them. Marinate the fish for an hour at room temperature, covered.

Remove the fish from the marinade and grill over a medium fire until the fish flakes easily, 8 to 10 minutes, turning often.

To serve, place the fish on individual plates, sprinkle the parsley over the fish, and garnish the plate with the lemon wedges.

Rum-Cured Hawaiian Salmon with Thai Pepper–Mint Chutney

SERVES: 4

HEAT SCALE: Hot

Some fish, before smoking, are treated with a liquid cure, a mixture of various ingredients that helps in the preservation process. This cure is both sweet and hot. For the chutney, fresh Thai chiles are available in Asian markets. Serve on a bed of white rice with the chutney on the side.

Hot Rum Cure

¼ cup dark rum

1 tablespoon brown sugar

1 teaspoon vegetable oil

2 teaspoons chopped fresh mint

2 teaspoons peeled and chopped
  fresh ginger

½ teaspoon ground habanero chile

4 salmon steaks

2 cups cooked white rice

Thai Pepper–Mint Chutney

2½ cups diced fresh mango

1 small red bell pepper, stemmed,
  seeded, and diced

½ cup thinly sliced red onion

¼ cup golden raisins

4 Thai chiles (*prik kee nu*) or 2
  serrano chiles, stemmed and
  chopped,

1 cup dry white wine

¼ cup red wine vinegar

2 teaspoons honey

6 whole peppercorns

2 tablespoons coarsely chopped fresh
  mint

To make the cure, combine the ingredients in a bowl. Allow the mixture to sit for 30 minutes to blend the flavors. Place the steaks in a glass dish and brush the cure on both sides. Cover and marinate for 4 hours in the refrigerator.

To make the chutney, combine all the ingredients, except the mint, in a saucepan and bring to a boil over high heat. Decrease the heat to medium and simmer for about 15 minutes until the fruits and vegetables are soft. Remove the mango, pepper, onion, and chiles and simmer the sauce until the liquid is reduced to a syrup, about 15 minutes. Return the fruit and vegetables and simmer for an additional 5 minutes. Allow to cool and add the mint.

Place the salmon steaks in a grill basket with handles. Grill the salmon over a medium fire until it flakes, about 15 minutes, turning occasionally.

To serve, place a scoop of rice on individual plates, top with the fish, and serve the chutney on the side.

❦ Chile-Grilled Scallops with Coconut-Mint Chutney

SERVES: 4 to 6
HEAT SCALE: Medium

The chutney is a nice and spicy accompaniment to the creamy taste of the scallops. We love habanero chiles in it, but use a serrano for less heat and a slightly different flavor. Serve with the Nutty Rice Pilaf (p. 85) and our Calypso Grilled Mango (p. 173) for dessert.

Hollywood BBQ

❦ Advice from Jonathan Winters: "Always wear gloves. Don't pretend to be from Calcutta and try to walk on the coals because it doesn't work!"

❦ The price of hardwoods such as oak and mesquite in southern California reached $400 a cord in 1999.

❦ Comedian Jeff Foxworthy says that you may be a redneck if you've ever tried spam on the grill.

❦ According to Walter Matthau's publicist, the star always marinates his steaks before grilling and plays Mozart while grilling.

❦ Former Monkee Micky Dolentz advises smoking meats first and then finishing them off on the grill.

Coconut-Mint Chutney

1 cup grated fresh coconut, or 1½ cups flaked

¼ cup freshly squeezed lemon juice

½ cup chopped onion

¼ cup peeled and chopped fresh ginger

1 habanero chile or serrano chile, stemmed, seeded, and minced

½ teaspoon salt

1 tablespoon vegetable oil

1 teaspoon mustard seeds

½ cup chopped fresh mint

2 pounds scallops

¼ cup vegetable oil

2 tablespoons ground New Mexican red chile

Salt and freshly ground black pepper

To make the chutney, combine the coconut and the lemon juice in a blender or food processor and purée until smooth. Add the onion, ginger, chiles, and salt and blend, adding enough water to make a smooth paste. Heat the oil in a skillet over medium heat, add the mustard seeds, and fry until they begin to sizzle. Add the coconut paste and let it heat through. Remove from heat and let it cool, then stir in the mint.

Blanch the scallops in boiling water for 2½ minutes. Drain and pat dry. In a bowl, toss the scallops in the oil. Sprinkle the scallops with the chile, salt, and pepper, and toss well to coat evenly. Thread the scallops on skewers and grill over medium-hot fire until they are golden brown on the outside and opaque throughout, 5 to 6 minutes, turning occasionally.

Serve the scallops with some of the chutney drizzled over them and additional chutney on the side.

 # Gingered and Grilled Shrimp Salad with Crispy Red Chile–Dusted Eggroll Strips

(pictured in photo section)

SERVES: 4

HEAT SCALE: Medium

The marinade in this recipe also doubles as the dressing for the salad. We use a commercial 5-spice powder that is available in Asian markets. We like to serve this salad with shrimp that is hot off the grill, but it can also be prepared ahead and served chilled. This is a meal in itself, so treat yourself and serve it with a dry white wine.

Gingered Shrimp Marinade and Dressing

¼ cup vegetable oil

¼ cup peanut oil

6 tablespoons rice wine vinegar

6 small Thai chiles (*prik kee nu*) or serrano chiles, stemmed and minced

2 tablespoons peeled and minced fresh ginger

1 tablespoon chopped green onion, green and white parts

1 tablespoon dry sherry

1 teaspoon 5-spice powder

1 teaspoon soy sauce

½ teaspoon sesame oil

---

24 shrimp, shelled and deveined, tails off

Vegetable oil, for frying

4 eggroll wrappers, cut into ¼-inch strips

Ground red New Mexican chile

4 loose handfuls of mixed baby greens or leaf lettuce

4 slices red onion

To make the marinade, combine all the ingredients in a blender or food processor and purée until smooth. Place in a bowl and allow to sit at room temperature for 1 to 2 hours.

Strain the marinade, saving both the solids and the liquid. Mix the solids with 3 tablespoons of the reserved liquid and brush on the shrimp. Place in a bowl and marinate in the refrigerator for 2 hours, or 1 hour at room temperature.

Pour the oil in a deep-fat fryer or wok to a depth of 2 inches and heat until hot, about 375°. Add the eggroll strips in batches and fry for 30 seconds, until crisp. Remove the strips from the oil, drain on paper towels, and sprinkle with the ground red chile.

Place the shrimp in a vegetable basket and grill over a medium-hot fire for about 6 minutes or until they are pink and opaque, shaking the shrimp often so that they get evenly cooked.

To serve, toss the greens with the reserved marinade liquid and divide between chilled salad plates. Arrange the sliced onion over the salads and top with the shrimp. Garnish the salads with the crispy strips and serve.

Sweet and Hot Shrimp with Jalapeño-Cilantro Couscous

SERVES: 4
HEAT SCALE: Medium

A staple in North Africa, couscous is wheat in granular form that is usually steamed. It is often combined with meats or vegetables. We, of course, have added chiles to it. The marinade is quite sweet—but works well with the shrimp. Interestingly, this is a re-creation of a dish Nancy was served in the British Virgin Islands.

Sweet and Hot Coconut Marinade

¼ cup firmly packed brown sugar
1 teaspoon ground habanero chile
2 teaspoons chopped fresh thyme, or
   ½ teaspoon dried thyme
2 tablespoons honey
¼ cup coconut milk
3 tablespoons vegetable oil
1 tablespoon freshly squeezed lime
   juice

24 shrimp, shelled and deveined,
   tails on

Jalapeño-Cilantro Couscous

1 tablespoon vegetable oil
2 cloves garlic, minced
2 shallots, chopped

1 jalapeño chile, stemmed, seeded,
   and minced
1 teaspoon dried thyme
1 cup couscous
2 cups chicken broth
2 tablespoons chopped fresh cilantro
1 tablespoon chopped chives
Salt and freshly ground black pepper

Kebabs

1 green or red bell pepper, stemmed,
   seeded, and cut into wedges
1 small onion, cut and separated into
   wedges
3 to 4 jalapeño chiles, stemmed,
   seeded, and cut into slivers
8 cherry tomatoes
Chopped fresh cilantro, for garnish

To make the marinade, combine the brown sugar, chile, thyme, honey, and coconut milk, and mix well. Slowly whisk in the oil and add the lime juice. Place the shrimp in a bowl and cover them with the marinade. Be sure to coat them well. Cover and marinate the shrimp for 1 hour at room temperature.

To make the couscous, heat the oil in a pan over medium heat, add the garlic, shallots, and jalapeño, and sauté until soft. Stir in the thyme. Place the couscous in a bowl. In a separate pan, bring the chicken broth to a boil over high heat. Pour over the couscous, flake with a fork, and let sit, covered, for 15 minutes. Drain off any excess liquid. Add the shallot mixture, cilantro, and chives, and toss to mix well. Season with salt and pepper and keep warm.

Remove the shrimp from the marinade. Thread the shrimp on skewers alternating with the vegetables. Grill the shrimp over a medium fire, basting frequently with the marinade until pink and opaque, 6 to 8 minutes, turning occasionally.

To serve, spoon the couscous onto a serving platter. Lay the kebabs over the couscous and serve.

NINE

The Meatless Grill with Elevated Heat Levels of All Kinds

IT'S NOT NICE to fool father carnivore, but it happens in this chapter. Dave remembers getting bamboozled by *seitan* than tasted exactly like beef in a Thai salad, and Nancy, who devilishly devised the recipes in this chapter, insists that neither meat lovers nor vegetarians will be disappointed with meatless on the grill. "Meatless doesn't have to mean flavorless," she notes, "and by using chiles and spices, you don't miss the meat and its attendant fat."

We carnivores and omnivores have noted the increasing interest in meatless cooking, and Dave is even the coauthor of two hot and spicy meatless cookbooks. Just note the fanatic enthusiasm for veggie burgers. In 1997, Gardenburger sales were $18 million and just a year later topped $55 million. Obviously veggie burgers are going mainstream, and they are excellent when grilled.

There are several reasons why grilling vegetables is better than boiling

Grilling evaporates some of the water in a vegetable, concentrating the flavor. High, dry heat caramelizes natural plant sugars, heightening a vegetable's sweetness. Unlike boiling, which removes flavor from vegetables, grilling seems to intensify their natural taste.

—Steven Raichlen, *The Barbecue Bible*

or steaming them. First, they lose fewer vitamins when grilled as opposed to other cooking techniques. Also, grilling and smoking vegetables seem to concentrate the flavors instead of boiling them off, and by using vinaigrettes with herbs and spices, you can gain additional flavor.

Vegetables that work best on the grill are the softer and less dense ones, such as peppers, mushrooms, onions, squash, ears of corn, and eggplants. Don't try grilling rutabagas unless you parboil them first, as they are quite dense.

Potatoes can be cooked in several ways on the grill. They can be sliced or cut in chunks, parboiled, and grilled directly in a basket, placed with other vegetable kebabs on a skewer, or whole potatoes can be rubbed with olive oil, wrapped in aluminum foil, and placed in the coals of a charcoal fire to bake. Ears of corn can also be cooked in the coals, either in their shucks or shucked and wrapped in foil, but we prefer the method used in Grilled Corn with African Nitir Kebe (page 159).

One final note on veggies on the grill: Most of them need some olive oil rubbed over them so they maintain their moisture and don't dry out on the grill.

 # Grilled Green Chile Cheese Tamales with Avocado Cream

MAKES:	5 to 7 tamales
HEAT SCALE:	Medium

Oh no, not a grilled tamale! But it works—if you can keep the corn husks from burning. And for that, be armed with a spray bottle filled with water. These tamales can be served as an entrée or as a side dish. You can tie the tamales together with string or with a thin strip of corn husk. The masa mix is available in Hispanic markets.

The Tamales
10 to 14 dried corn husks
½ cup cornmeal
⅓ cup milk
2 tablespoons butter

1 tablespoon instant masa mix
1 tablespoon sugar
1 teaspoon salt
½ cup whole corn kernels

Green Chile Cheese Filling

6 to 8 green New Mexican chiles, roasted, peeled, stemmed, seeded, and cut into strips
⅓ cup finely chopped onion
⅓ cup chopped black olives
6 ounces *asadero* or Monterey Jack cheese, coarsely grated

Avocado Cream

2 avocados, peeled and chopped
2 jalapeño chiles, stemmed, seeded, and chopped
2 tablespoons chopped onion
1 tablespoon freshly squeezed lemon juice
2 teaspoons chopped fresh cilantro
¼ teaspoon garlic salt

Sour cream, for garnish
Chopped fresh cilantro, for garnish

To make the tamales, place the corn husks in a large bowl of water and weigh them down with a plate. Allow them to soak for 30 minutes or until soft.

Combine the cornmeal, milk, butter, masa, sugar, and salt in a saucepan and simmer over medium heat for 2 or 3 minutes. Remove from the heat, let cool, then add the corn.

Drain the husks, pat dry with paper towels, and lay on a flat surface. Place 2 together, making sure they overlap a little. Spread some of the cornmeal mixture on a husk, cover with chile strips, then onion, olives, and cheese. Place another layer of the cornmeal on top, wrap the husks over the top, and tie at both ends. Repeat until you have finished the filling and made 5 to 7 packets.

Arrange the tamales around the edge of a high-heat grill. Grill until the filling sets, 45 to 60 minutes, turning occasionally and spraying with water to keep the husks from burning.

To make the avocado cream, place all the ingredients in a blender or food processor and purée until smooth.

To serve, slice open the tamales, spoon in the avocado cream, top with a dollop of sour cream, and sprinkle with cilantro.

Mixed Mediterranean Herbed Vegetables with Penne Pasta and Feta Cheese

(pictured in photo section)

SERVES: 4 to 6
HEAT SCALE: Mild

Here is a dish that Nancy likes to prepare towards the end of the summer when fresh vegetables are in abundance and she doesn't want to heat up the kitchen with a hot stove. Use the tomatoes as a base and vary the types of vegetables for a different pasta taste. Begin the meal with a crisp Caesar salad and finish it with a cool dish of ice cream.

2 tomatoes, halved
1 small zucchini, halved lengthwise
1 yellow bell pepper, stemmed, seeded, and cut into quarters
1 red onion, thickly sliced

The Herbed Marinade
⅓ cup olive oil
1 tablespoon minced fresh oregano, or 1 teaspoon dried oregano
2 cloves garlic, minced or pressed
1 teaspoon ground cayenne chile

The Pasta
4 cups cooked penne pasta
1 tablespoon crushed piquín chile or other small, hot chile
1 tablespoon chopped fresh Greek or domestic oregano, or 1 teaspoon dried oregano
2 tablespoons chopped fresh Italian parsley
2 teaspoons red wine vinegar
1 (6½-ounce) jar marinated artichoke hearts, drained
12 kalamata olives, pitted and sliced or slivered
Salt and freshly ground black pepper
1 cup crumbled feta cheese

Place the vegetables in a large bowl. To prepare the marinade, in a small bowl, whisk the oil, oregano, garlic, and cayenne together and pour over the vegetables. Marinate the vegetables for 1 hour at room temperature.

Remove the vegetables from the marinade and reserve 2 tablespoons of the marinade. Place the vegetables in a grill basket and grill over a medium fire until the vegetables are slightly cooked but still a little firm, about 7 minutes. Be sure to shake the basket so that the vegetables are evenly grilled. Remove the vegetables from the basket and chop them. Place the vegetables, and any liquid released while chopping, in a bowl.

Toss the hot pasta with the reserved marinade, chile, oregano, parsley, and vinegar. Add the vegetables, artichoke hearts, and olives, and toss again. To serve, season with salt and pepper and top with the cheese.

Orange-Chipotle–Glazed Portabello Mushroom Steaks

SERVES: 4
HEAT SCALE: Mild

Here's a hunka hunka burning mushroom. It is amazing how portabellos resemble meat in their texture and response to grilling. Some people think that the flavor of the portabello is too intense by itself, so feel free to make mushroom "cheeseburgers" by melting cheese over the mushrooms and serving them on buns brushed with olive oil and then grilled, accompanied by the Grilled Mediterranean Potato Salad (p. 168) or a tossed green salad. Incidentally, portabellos (also portobello and portobella) are the same as cremini mushrooms, just more mature.

Orange-Chipotle Glaze
½ cup freshly squeezed orange juice
2 tablespoons honey
2 chipotle chiles in adobo
1 teaspoon dried Mexican or other oregano

½ teaspoon garlic powder
⅛ teaspoon saffron dissolved in 2 tablespoons boiling water

4 large portabello mushrooms

Place all the ingredients for the glaze in a blender or food processor and purée until smooth. Thoroughly wash the mushrooms, pat dry, and cut the stems off flush with the cap.

Brush each of the portabellos with the glaze and let sit for 30 minutes. Place the mushrooms on the grill, stem side up. Grill over a medium fire for 2 minutes, then turn. Brush on more glaze, grill for 2 minutes, and turn again. Reglaze the mushrooms and grill for 2 more minutes.

To serve, brush the mushrooms with the remaining glaze and place on individual plates.

Grilled Tangerine Tofu

SERVES: 4 to 6
HEAT SCALE: Medium

Since tofu was invented in China, it is perfectly appropriate to grill it after a good soak-ing in an Asian marinade such as this one. And it does absorb a marinade! Tofu comes in different styles—soft, regular, firm, and extra-firm. The firmer ones are best for grilling, but it is still critical to remove as much liquid from the tofu as possible. The 5-spice powder is a commercial blend available in Asian markets. Serve these tofu kebabs over plain rice or soft Chinese noodles.

1 (1-pound) package firm tofu
2 cups cooked white rice or noodles

Tangerine Marinade
⅓ cup tangerine juice
2 tablespoons rice wine vinegar

1 tablespoon soy sauce
1 teaspoon grated tangerine zest
1 teaspoon hoisin sauce
1 teaspoon crushed red chile, such as
   New Mexican
½ teaspoon 5-spice powder

Place a thick layer of paper towels on a plate. Place the tofu on the towels and cover with another thick layer of towels. Place a heavy skillet on top of the paper towels and let sit for an hour to remove excess moisture.

To make the marinade, combine all the ingredients in a bowl. Cut the tofu into 1-inch cubes. Place the tofu in a nonreactive bowl, pour the mari-nade over the tofu, cover, and refrigerate for 3 hours.

Thread the tofu cubes onto skewers. Grill over a medium-hot fire for 5

Varying Vegetable Grilling Hints from the Experts

Resist the temptation to parboil or partially cook in the microwave oven any vegetable before grilling. Both techniques alter the texture of the vegetable, resulting in a mushy, inferior dish.

—A. Cort Sinnes, *Gas Grill Gourmet*

minutes, turn, cook another 5 minutes, until the outside is slightly crispy and brown.

To serve, mound the rice in a large bowl and top with the tofu.

 ## Pungent Pizza on the Grill

MAKES: 1 (12-inch) or 2 individual pizzas
HEAT SCALE: Mild to medium

In this recipe we attempt to re-create the wonderful thin-crust pizza from wood-fired ovens for preparation in your very own backyard. Our homemade crust has something that Pizza Doodle Express does not: chile. But if you're lazy and don't want to make your own dough, you can use a 12-inch, prebaked pizza shell. You can also easily make the dough in your bread machine. It is very important to have a clean grill for this recipe, as any residue on the grill will give the crust an off flavor. Why not make both toppings and divide the pizza?

The Chile Dough
1 cup warm water
1 teaspoon sugar
1 teaspoon yeast
1½ cups all-purpose flour
¾ teaspoon salt
2 teaspoons crushed red chile
Freshly ground black pepper
2 tablespoons olive oil, plus extra for brushing

Puttanesca Topping
3 cups chopped fresh cherry or plum tomatoes
2 tablespoons chopped capers
2 tablespoons chopped niçoise olives
1 tablespoon chopped fresh basil
2 teaspoons crushed red chile
1 cup grated Parmigiano-Reggiano or pecorino-Romano cheese
Garlic salt
Olive oil, for sprinkling

Southwest Green Chile Topping
8 New Mexican green chiles, roasted, peeled and halved lengthwise
1 cup grated mozzarella cheese
½ cup grated provolone cheese
Olive oil, for sprinkling

To make the dough, combine the water and sugar in a bowl and stir in the yeast. Let stand for 10 minutes until it becomes foamy.

In a large bowl, combine the flour, salt, chile, and pepper. Make a well in the flour and pour in the yeast water and olive oil. Stir until almost mixed, turn onto a floured board, and knead until the dough is smooth and elastic.

Place the dough in a lightly oiled bowl and cover with plastic wrap. Place in a draft-free location at a temperature between 70° and 85°, and let rise until doubled, about 1½ hours.

Punch down the dough and divide into 2 balls. If preparing ahead of time, cover with plastic wrap, and place in the refrigerator until ready to use. Bring the dough back to room temperature and then proceed with the recipe.

Roll out each portion into a round or oval pizza or do it free-form. If it will fit on your grill, you can also combine the balls into one and make one large pizza.

Heat a gas grill to hot. If using charcoal, bank the coals to one side, creating a hot side and a warm side.

Brush each of the pizzas with olive oil and gently drape, oil side down, on a hot grill. Within a minute or two, the dough will start to rise and bubbles will appear. Gently lift an end to see that the underside is browned and has grill marks. Immediately invert the crust onto a pan. If using a gas grill, turn it to low.

Brush the dough with additional oil.

To make the puttanesca topping, place the tomatoes on the cooked side of the pizza, sprinkle the capers, olives, basil, chile, and cheese over the top. Shake a little garlic salt and sprinkle some olive oil over the top.

To make the Southwest topping, lay the green chile strips over the cooked side. Top with the cheeses and a sprinkling of the olive oil. Slide the pizza(s) back onto the grill. Cover and cook, rotating once or twice until the toppings are heated through and the crust is browned, about 5 minutes on the cooler part of the grill.

Remove the pizzas from the grill, cut into eighths, and serve.

Grilled Corn with African Nitir Kebe

(pictured in photo section)

SERVES: 4

HEAT SCALE: Hot

Nitir kebe *is Ethiopian spiced butter and is an ingredient in many of that country's dishes. It certainly gives an exotic twist to a summertime favorite in the U.S.A. Be sure to buy ears of corn with some of the stalk attached for a great handle. The spiced butter freezes easily. Serve this corn with any grilled meat, especially steak, or any of the rib recipes in chapter 6.*

Nitir Kebe

1 pound unsalted butter, at room temperature

1 tablespoon crushed African bird peppers, or chiltepíns, piquíns, or ground cayenne chile

2 shallots, minced

1 tablespoon peeled and grated fresh ginger

2 cloves garlic, minced

1 teaspoon ground cloves

1 teaspoon ground cinnamon

1 teaspoon ground cardamom

1½ teaspoons ground turmeric

4 ears corn, husks and stalks attached

Beat together all the nitir kebe ingredients. Let sit for 1 hour to blend the flavors.

Remove any dried, brownish husks from the corn. Pull the husks back, but don't tear them off. Remove the silk. Soak the ears in cold water for 30 minutes to prevent the husks from burning.

Spread some of the butter mixture on the corn kernels. Pull the husks back up over the ears, and secure with a string or a strip of corn husk.

Place on the grill over a low fire, fairly far from the heat, and grill, turning often, for about 15 minutes. It's a good idea to have a spray bottle with water handy in case the husks start to burn.

To serve, pull down one side of the husks and arrange the ears on a platter. Top with a pat of the butter. The remainder of the butter can be frozen for future use.

Barbecue Restaurant Rules

Barbecue lovers love to make barbecue rules. Never go in a barbecue joint that has a gas pump outside. Never go in a barbecue joint that sells hamburgers. Never go in a barbecue joint that's nicer looking than your house. Never eat at a barbecue joint that has its own T-shirts. But for every rule there is an exception.

—Greg Johnson and Vince Staten, *Real Barbecue*

 # Grilled Jalapeño Polenta with Roasted Salsa Verde

SERVES: 4 to 6
HEAT SCALE: Medium

In chapter 2 we talked about roasted salsas, and here's a practical application of the concept. While we're at it, we'll add chiles to everything and even grill the polenta. Serve as an entrée with a vegetable and a salad, or as a side to grilled meat or chicken.

Grilled Jalapeño Polenta
1½ cups milk
1½ cups water
¾ cup coarse yellow cornmeal
½ cup grated Cheddar or Asiago
    cheese
2 jalapeño chiles, stemmed, seeded,
    and chopped
2 tablespoons grated onion
1 clove garlic, minced
Salt
3 tablespoons olive oil

Roasted Salsa Verde
1 pound fresh tomatillos, husks left
    on
1 small onion, quartered
4 jalapeño chiles
2 tablespoons freshly squeezed lime
    juice
1 teaspoon sugar
Salt
¼ cup chopped fresh cilantro

To make the polenta, bring the milk and water to a boil in a large saucepan over high heat. Slowly sprinkle the cornmeal into the liquid, stirring constantly. Decrease the heat to medium-low and continue to stir until the mixture is thick and starts to pull away from the pan. Quickly add the cheese, chiles, onion, garlic, and salt, stir well, and remove the pan from the heat.

Pour the polenta into a lightly oiled 10-inch cake or pie pan and allow to cool at room temperature. Cover and place in refrigerator for 3 hours until firm.

To make the salsa, place the tomatillos, onion, and chiles in a basket on the grill and roast until the vegetables are slightly blackened, shaking the basket often. Remove the vegetables from the basket and peel, but don't worry about removing all the peels from the chiles. Made sure to remove the stems and the seeds from the chiles. Place the vegetables, lime juice, and sugar into a blender or food processor and purée until smooth. Season with salt to taste and stir in the cilantro.

Clean the grill and brush it with oil. Slice the polenta into wedges, brush with the oil, and grill over a medium fire until they begin to brown, 8 to 12 minutes.

To serve, place the polenta wedges on a serving platter and top with the salsa.

Just Give Us a Time Machine and We'll Be There, Part 3

We arrived on the barbecue grounds at about ten o'clock. More than two thousand people had already arrived, some from a distance of forty to fifty miles. . . . A deep trench, three hundred feet long, had been dug. This trench was filled from end to end with glowing coals; and suspended over them on horizonal poles were the carcasses of forty animals—sheep, hogs, oxen, and deer—roasting over the slow fire. . . . It is claimed that this primitive method of preparation is the perfection of cookery, and that no meat tastes so sweet as that which is barbecued.

—Alexander Sweet and John Knox, *On a Mexican Mustang through Texas*, 1905

TEN

Super Spicy Sides
and Some Grilled Desserts

GRILLED AND BARBECUED FOODS seem to have recurrent side dishes like potato salad, coleslaw, baked beans, and the like. They're all usually prepared in the kitchen and have nothing to do with the grill. We decided not to include those traditional sides because it's time for a side revolution. Let's start using the grill and smoker for side dishes. Even our desserts are grilled! Okay, partially grilled.

In the summer we love to create dishes from what we can immediately find in our gardens and thereby completely bypass the kitchen by using the grill. As noted earlier, chiles are routinely roasted on the grill and then peeled, and when you use the same technique with tomatoes and onions, you can make a simple but delicious grilled salsa. Whole heads of garlic can be dipped in olive oil and then grilled. The soft cloves are then pushed out of the peels and spread over toasted bread with goat cheese and a little chili powder—a spectacular tasting but simple side dish. And if you wanted to place the goat cheese and grilled garlic on fresh bread, and then grill it, we wouldn't discourage you.

A favorite side dish is salads, and they also can be grilled or partially grilled. The concept is not new. For centuries in Tuscany, heads of endive have been grilled with a little olive oil and salt. Spinach can be wilted on the grill for use in salads, accompanied by grilled tomatoes, mushrooms, onions, leeks, and bell peppers that are all chopped together.

Pieces of fruit grilled in a basket or on skewers make a great accompaniment to grilled fish, and can also be part of a wonderful dessert. The sugars in the fruits caramelize and add sweetness. Some of our favorite grilled fruits are pineapples, mangoes, bananas, and peaches. These grilled fruits are great mixed with yogurt or ice cream, or even with just a dollop of whipped cream over them.

 # Grilled Panzanella Salad with Hot Sundried Tomato Dressing

SERVES: 4 to 6
HEAT SCALE: Medium

Yes, you can grill some salad ingredients! This modified Italian recipe uses leftover bread: Grilling the stale bread keeps it from getting soggy in the salad. It is a nice accompaniment to grilled meats and poultry. Be careful: The heat level builds as you eat.

Hot Sundried Tomato Dressing
½ cup dry white wine
6 dry-packed sundried tomatoes, finely chopped
½ cup olive oil
¼ cup balsamic vinegar
3 cloves garlic, minced
3 small fresh red chiles, such as serrano or jalapeño, stemmed, seeded, and finely chopped
1 tablespoon chopped fresh Italian parsley

Garlic Brushing Oil
¼ cup olive oil
4 large cloves garlic, minced
1 teaspoon ground cayenne chile

12 cherry tomatoes, halved
4 (1-inch-thick) slices, day-old Italian bread, crusts removed
1 stalk of celery, including the leaves, finely sliced
½ cup stuffed green olives, halved
1 large red leaf lettuce leaf, finely sliced

Grated Parmesan cheese, for garnish

To make the dressing, bring the wine to a simmer in a small saucepan over medium heat. Add the tomatoes, remove the pan from the heat, and let cool.

In a bowl, combine the remaining dressing ingredients, add the tomatoes and wine, and let sit for 1 hour at room temperature to allow the flavors to blend.

To make the brushing oil, in a bowl, whisk together the olive oil, garlic, and cayenne. Toss the cherry tomatoes in the mixture and marinate for 30 minutes. Remove the tomatoes from the oil and reserve the oil.

In a grill basket, grill the cherry tomatoes over a medium fire until just heated, about 2 minutes. Brush the bread with the oil and grill for 2 or 3 minutes on each side, until lightly marked. Cut the bread into ½- to ¾-inch cubes.

In a bowl, toss the remaining salad ingredients together with the grilled tomatoes and bread cubes. Top with the dressing and toss. Garnish with grated cheese, and serve immediately.

 # Grilled Artichokes Stuffed with Serrano-Cilantro Aioli

SERVES: 6 to 8
HEAT SCALE: Medium

This is an extremely versatile dish that can be prepared ahead of time and thrown back on the grill as it is heating up. It can be served either warm or cold. To take a shortcut with the aioli, we have used a prepared mayonnaise as the base.

You Don't Need a Time Machine for This BBQ Trip

Unlike other barbecue hot spots like Kansas City and Memphis, Texas has no capital of 'que. Instead, it's a title shared throughout this Barbecue Belt region. Most places in this area share a similar cooking style, serve up their plates with sides of pinto beans, coleslaw, potato salad, and white bread, and offer squirt bottles of tomatoey barbecue sauce on every table. They also offer you a chance to eat with small-town Texans, from bankers to bricklayers, who frequent these little joints every day at noon.

—Paris Permenter and John Bigley, *Texas Barbecue*

4 small fresh artichokes

2 lemon slices

Cayenne Marinade

¼ cup rice wine vinegar

2 tablespoons olive oil

1 teaspoon ground cayenne chile

Serrano-Cilantro Aioli

1 cup mayonnaise

2 tablespoons chopped fresh cilantro

2 teaspoons minced serrano chiles

1 teaspoon freshly squeezed lime
    juice

¼ teaspoon cumin seeds

Cut the artichokes in half vertically and scoop out the center leaves and the "fur" of the choke. Immediately squeeze some lemon juice over the center and cut leaves to keep the artichoke from discoloring. Poach the artichokes in boiling water until the leaves just start to come off easily, about 20 minutes. Drain the artichokes.

To make the marinade, combine all the ingredients in a bowl. Drizzle the marinade over the artichokes and marinate, covered for a couple of hours at room temperature.

To make the aioli, combine all the ingredients and allow to sit at room temperature for 30 minutes or more to blend the flavors.

Grill the artichokes in a vegetable basket over a medium-low fire for 10 minutes or until the heart is tender.

To serve, place the artichokes on plates and place a dollop of the aioli in the center of each artichoke. Serve with additional aioli on the side.

And We'd Like to Sample Every One of 'Em

As if it's not bad enough that some people don't *understand* barbecue, there are actually some who balk at the thought of eating it. According to NPD, a market research firm in Rosemont, Illinois, that tracks such things, fewer than 2 percent of all American eating places can be defined as pure barbecue restaurants. By latest count [1998], that's 7,294, and to the people who see the act of sucking the sweet meat out of a gristly rib tip as uncivil and animalistic, 7,294 is enough.

—Connie McCabe, "KC BBQ"

Smoked Dijon-Broccoli Parmigiana

SERVES: 4
HEAT SCALE: Medium

No, we're not going to super-saturate this vegetable with smoke, but rather lightly flavor it with a little smoke dust. So don't fire up the meat smoker—use a gas or charcoal grill with some soaked wood chips like apple, oak, or pecan. You can also use a stove-top smoker for this dish and use smoke dust such as oak.

2 tablespoons olive oil
2 tablespoons balsamic vinegar or
    white wine
2 teaspoons crushed red chile
1 tablespoon Dijon mustard

¼ teaspoon ground white pepper
Pinch of salt
1 pound fresh broccoli
¼ cup grated Parmesan cheese

Combine all the ingredients except the broccoli and cheese in a bowl and mix well.

Slice each broccoli stalk in half lengthwise, cutting through the florets. Trim the stalks to 3 inches. Cut a shallow groove down the center of each stalk and remove the core.

Place the broccoli pieces in a shallow nonreactive dish, pour the marinade over them, and toss to coat. Marinate the broccoli, covered, for 30 minutes at room temperature.

Place the broccoli on the grill, cut side down. Brush with the remaining marinade. Cover and cook for 15 minutes or until just tender.

To serve, place the broccoli on a serving platter and sprinkle with the cheese.

The Kansas City Barbecue Society Judge's Oath

I solemnly swear to objectively and subjectively evaluate each barbecue meat that is presented to my eyes, my nose, and my palate. I accept my duty so that truth, justice, excellence in barbecue and the American Way of Life may be strengthened and preserved forever.

—Remus Powers, Ph.B. (a.k.a. Dr. of Barbecue, Ardie Davis)

Grilled Spring Asparagus with Spicy Lemon Mop *(pictured on photo section)*

SERVES: 4
HEAT SCALE: Mild

No, you can't use canned or frozen—it only works with fresh asparagus, so take advantage of those spring asparagus months. This is an excellent accompaniment to grilled seafood. You can find some of that in chapter 8.

Spicy Lemon Mop
3 tablespoons olive oil
2 tablespoons freshly squeezed
  lemon juice
2 serrano chiles, stemmed, seeded,
  and minced

2 cloves garlic, minced
2 teaspoons chopped fresh parsley or
  rosemary
Freshly ground black pepper

1 pound fresh asparagus

To make the mop, combine all the ingredients in a small bowl and mix well.

Cut off the tough stem ends of the asparagus, rinse, and place in a non-reactive, shallow bowl. Pour the mop over the asparagus and marinate, at room temperature, for 1 hour.

Grill the asparagus over medium heat for 2 minutes on each side or until tender but still crisp.

To serve, arrange the spears on a serving platter and brush with any remaining mop.

Barbecue Timing and Mixed Metaphors

Barbecue is any four-footed animal—be it a mouse or mastodon. . . . At it's best it is a fat steer, and it must be eaten within an hour of when it is cooked. For if ever the sun rises upon Barbecue, its flavor vanishes like Cinderella's silks . . . staler in the chill dawn than illicit love.

—William Allen White

Grilled Mediterranean Potato Salad with Yogurt-Cayenne Dressing

SERVES: 4
HEAT SCALE: Mild

A vegetable basket is the best way to grill the major ingredients for this salad. Toss the salad together just before serving or the warm potatoes will absorb all the dressing! You could also allow the potatoes to cool first.

Yogurt-Cayenne Dressing
¼ cup plain yogurt
1 tablespoon Dijon mustard
2 teaspoons cider vinegar
¼ teaspoon ground cayenne chile
Salt

6 small red potatoes, unpeeled, diced into eighths

1 small red onion, thickly sliced
2 tablespoons olive oil
½ cup chopped green New Mexican chile
2 tablespoons chopped fresh Italian parsley
⅓ cup sliced green onion, white and green parts

To make the dressing, combine all the ingredients, including salt to taste, and allow to sit at room temperature for 30 minutes to blend the flavors.

To make the salad, in a bowl, toss the potatoes and onions in the oil. Place the potatoes in a vegetable basket and place on the grill over a medium fire. Grill for about 15 minutes, shaking the basket often and watching for flare-ups from the olive oil. Add the onion and grill for 5 more minutes. Remove from the grill and chop the onions.

In a bowl, combine the potatoes, onions, and chile with the dressing and toss until coated. Add the remaining ingredients, toss to mix, and serve.

North African Grilled Eggplant Salad with Garlic-Cayenne Dressing

SERVES: 6
HEAT SCALE: Mild

Eggplant is one of the best vegetables to grill. This salad is the same basic idea as a potato salad, but the flavor is totally different. As a variation, add one roasted and chopped tomato.

1 cucumber, thinly sliced
1 small red onion, thinly sliced
2 small eggplants, halved
2 poblano chiles, stemmed, seeded, and halved lengthwise
1 cup 1-inch pieces red bell pepper
1 onion, cut into 8 wedges
2 tablespoons olive oil

¼ teaspoon salt
⅛ teaspoon freshly ground black pepper
2 tablespoons red wine or balsamic vinegar
½ teaspoon ground cayenne chile
1 tablespoon finely chopped fresh parsley

Garlic-Cayenne Dressing
1 teaspoon cumin seeds
1 clove garlic, chopped
1 tablespoon olive oil

3 tablespoons cider vinegar
1 tablespoon brown sugar
½ teaspoon salt
Chopped fresh parsley, for garnish

Cover the cucumber and onion slices with ice water in a bowl. Gently squeeze the slices to bruise them lightly. Cover and chill for 30 minutes to 1 hour.

Lightly brush the eggplant halves, chiles, bell pepper, and onion wedges with the oil. Place them in a vegetable basket on the grill over a medium fire. Cover the grill, open the vents, and grill until the eggplant is browned and soft when pressed, 15 to 20 minutes. Be sure to shake the basket to cook the vegetables evenly.

To make the dressing, in a small skillet, sauté the cumin seeds for 20 seconds over medium-low heat, stirring constantly. Add the garlic and oil and sauté for an additional 2 or 3 minutes. Add the remaining dressing ingredients, stir, and quickly remove the skillet from the heat.

Coarsely chop the eggplant and chiles and toss in a bowl along with the other grilled vegetables and the dressing. Drain the cucumber and onion and place in a bowl with the cider vinegar, brown sugar, and salt. Mix well.

To serve, spoon the eggplant mixture onto a serving platter and top with the cucumber mixture. Garnish with the parsley.

 # Chile and Dried Cherry Chocolate Dessert

SERVES: 6
HEAT SCALE: Mild

This layered dessert is unique in that it can be cooked on the grill. Since it does have chile in it, it can become an honorary member of the barbecue inferno. Don't worry: Ancho powder is quite mild and has a nice raisiny flavor. The finished dessert has a cake-like topping and a chocolate syrup on the bottom. You can serve it with the Nutmeg Whipped Cream (p. 172).

Suggested Fruits for Grilling

Banana	Sliced in half lengthwise
Mango	½-inch-thick slices
Orange	Single sections
Papaya	½-inch-thick slices
Peach	½-inch-thick slices
Pear	½-inch-thick slices
Pineapple	½-inch-thick rings
Strawberry	Sliced in half

The Pudding

1 cup all-purpose flour
⅔ cup granulated sugar
2 tablespoons unsweetened cocoa
1 tablespoon ground ancho chile
2 teaspoons baking powder
½ teaspoon ground cinnamon
½ teaspoon salt
Pinch of ground nutmeg
½ cup milk
¼ cup dried cherries, soaked in
    water to plump
2 tablespoons melted butter or
    margarine
1 teaspoon vanilla extract

The Topping

½ cup firmly packed brown sugar
¼ cup granulated sugar
3 tablespoons unsweetened cocoa
1 teaspoon vanilla extract
½ teaspoon salt
1 cup boiling water

Rum Glaze

1 cup sugar
½ cup (1 stick) butter
¼ cup water
½ cup dark rum

Whipped cream, for topping

To make the pudding, sift all the dry ingredients into a large mixing bowl. Add the milk, cherries, butter, and vanilla, and mix until well blended. Pour into a well-greased, 9-inch square metal pan.

To make the topping, combine all the ingredients except the water in a bowl and spread over the pudding mixture. Slowly pour the boiling water over the top, but don't stir it in.

Heat a gas grill to low or bank 20 low-glowing coals on each side of the bottom of the grill unit. Place the cooking grill rack 4 to 6 inches above the coals. Place the baking pan in the center of the grill so that no part is directly over the coals. In a gas grill, light one burner and place the pan over the unlit burner. Cover and cook for 45 minutes. The pudding should be slightly crusty on top with a syrupy bottom.

To make the glaze, combine all the ingredients except the rum in a saucepan over medium heat and simmer for 5 to 10 minutes. Remove the pan from the heat, let cool slightly, and stir in the rum.

To serve, spoon the pudding into individual dishes, top with a dollop of whipped cream, and drizzle the rum glaze over the top.

Grilled Rum Bananas with Nutmeg Whipped Cream

SERVES: 4
HEAT SCALE: Mild

Remember this rule: The firmer the banana, the better it grills. You can start this dessert while eating the entrée, and it will be ready when you are. You can also use aluminum foil rather than the aluminum pan over the grill, if you wish.

½ cup firmly packed brown sugar

¼ cup dark rum

1 teaspoon soy sauce

2 teaspoons commercial fruit and habanero hot sauce

2 teaspoons freshly squeezed lime juice

2 teaspoons melted butter

4 small firm bananas, peeled and sliced in half lengthwise

½ cup heavy whipping cream

2 tablespoons granulated sugar

1 teaspoon rum

Grated nutmeg, for garnish

In a bowl, combine the brown sugar, rum, soy sauce, hot sauce, lime juice, and butter.

Arrange the bananas in a single layer in a disposable aluminum pan and drizzle the rum mixture over the top. Set the pan on the grill over a medium fire, cover, and cook for 10 minutes, basting frequently with the sauce. Continue to grill until the bananas are glazed and tender, another 5 to 10 minutes.

Whip the cream, granulated sugar, and rum together in a cold bowl until stiff.

To serve, place the bananas on individual serving plates, drizzle a teaspoon of the remaining sauce over them, top with a dollop of whipped cream, and garnish with the grated nutmeg.

Calypso Grilled Mango

SERVES: 4

HEAT SCALE: Mild

Grilling caramelizes the sugar and honey in the sauce, making the fruit sweeter. This is obviously a dessert, but it can be served as a side dish to barbecued ribs, poultry, or fish. Other firm fruits will work, such as peaches or pineapple, but make sure that they are slightly underripe. It is difficult to grill ripe fruit.

Habanero Sauce
¼ cup butter
2 tablespoons freshly squeezed
   orange juice
2 teaspoons honey
½ teaspoon freshly squeezed lime
   juice
1 teaspoon grated orange zest

½ teaspoon coconut extract
½ teaspoon ground habanero chile

2 mangoes, slightly underripe
Toasted shredded coconut
Vanilla ice cream
Chopped macadamia nuts, for
   garnish

To make the sauce, combine the ingredients in a saucepan and simmer over low heat for 10 minutes. Remove the pan from the heat and let cool.

Peel the mangoes and remove the flesh by cutting away from the seed on the flat side of each fruit. You should have 2 large slices of fruit from each mango.

Brush the mango slices with some of the sauce and let stand for 5 minutes. Place the mango slices in a grill basket, and grill over a low fire for 4 to 6 minutes, until lightly browned and glazed. Turn often and baste with the sauce.

To serve, sprinkle the coconut over 4 serving plates, place a mango slice and a scoop of ice cream over the coconut, drizzle the remaining sauce over the fruit and the ice cream, and garnish with the macadamia nuts.

Grand Marnier, Ancho, and Chocolate Dessert Kebabs

SERVES: 2 to 4
HEAT SCALE: Mild

A purchased cake works well in this recipe; you don't have to go to the trouble of baking one from scratch. You can substitute Kahlúa or other coffee liqueur for the Grand Marnier, and you can use other fruits, such as pineapple.

Grand Marnier Sauce

1 (8-ounce) milk chocolate bar
1 cup heavy cream
¼ cup Grand Marnier or other
    orange flavored liqueur
1½ teaspoon ground ancho chile

1 ripe peach, peeled, cut into wedges
1 slightly underripe banana, cut into
    1-inch cubes
12 (1-inch) cubes angel food cake
Grated orange zest and fresh mint
    leaves, for garnish

To make the sauce, break up the chocolate and melt it in a saucepan over very low heat. Add the cream, stir well, then remove the pan from the heat. Add the Grand Marnier and chile and stir well.

Using two skewers together to prevent flopping, thread the peaches, bananas, and cake onto the skewers.

Grill the kebabs directly over medium heat for 1 to 3 minutes on each side, until the cake is toasted, turning once.

To serve, remove the fruit and cake from the skewers and place on individual plates. Drizzle with the chocolate sauce, and garnish with orange zest and mint leaves.

Grilled Peach Halves Stuffed with Cheese and Chipotle-Raspberry Purée

(pictured in photo section)

SERVES: 4
HEAT SCALE: Mild

Do not peel the peaches. The chipotle chile adds a nice hint of heat and smoke to thisspectacular way to end a great meal off the grill. An interesting variation is to substitute Stilton cheese for the goat cheese.

The Peaches
6 tablespoons raspberry vinegar
4 tablespoons firmly packed brown sugar
4 tablespoons freshly squeezed lime juice
4 firm ripe peaches, halved vertically and pitted
Finely chopped walnuts, for garnish

Cheese Filling
4 tablespoons cream cheese, at room temperature
4 tablespoons goat cheese, at room temperature

Chipotle-Raspberry Purée
3 cups frozen raspberries
2 teaspoons freshly squeezed lemon juice
2 tablespoons granulated sugar
1 teaspoon ground chipotle chile

—Barbecue Philosophy—
It's a Social Thing

My sense is that once people get involved [in a barbecue cook-off] there's this camaraderie that develops, regardless of who you are. It becomes a little barbecue community. But I'm an idealist, so I may be projecting what I want to happen. I think that when people are enjoying food together that common denominator can do a lot of bonding that can't happen any other way. That's one reason I love barbecue.

—Ardie Davis, *The Great BBQ Sauce Book*

To prepare the peaches, combine the vinegar, brown sugar, and lime juice in a small saucepan and simmer for 10 minutes over medium heat, until slightly thickened. Remove the pan from the heat, let cool, add the peaches, and marinate for an additional 20 minutes.

To prepare the cheese filling, mix the cheeses together in a small bowl and let sit at room temperature for 30 minutes to blend the flavors.

To make the purée, slightly thaw the raspberries. Place all the ingredients in a blender or food processor and purée until smooth.

Remove the peaches from the marinade and place them in a grill basket with handles. Grill them flesh side down over a medium-hot fire for 2 to 3 minutes, until the grill marks show. Turn and grill until the peaches are soft.

To serve, spoon some of the raspberry purée on a dessert plate and place 2 peach halves cut side up on the sauce. Put a dollop of cheese in the center of each half and top with additional purée. Garnish with the walnuts.

Barbecue and Grilling Glossary

Baby Back Ribs. Tender ribs from a young hog cut from the loin or back section.

Barbacoa. The Spanish word for barbecue, but generally refers to the head of a cow that is wrapped in cloth and cooked slowly in a pit.

Barbecue. As a verb, in the most general sense, to cook outdoors. More specifically, to smoke meats by indirect heat and then to finish them with sauces. As a noun, it means the entire unit used to grill foods and an outdoor cooking event.

Barbecue Sauce. A condiment used to finish the barbecue after the meat is smoked.

Baste. To apply a mop, sop, or marinade during the grilling or smoking process.

Beef Back Ribs. Large ribs cut from the loin of the cow.

Beef Short Ribs. Thick ribs cut from the bottom end of the cow's rib cage.

Brisket. The chest muscle of a cow and one of the favorite cuts of Texas-style barbecue.

Burnt Ends. The blackened, crisp, fatty portion of the tapered end of a smoked brisket. A favorite in Kansas City barbecue.

Cabrito. Spanish word for young goat.

Country-Style Spareribs. Meaty sections from the rib end of the pork loin.

Drip Pan. An aluminum pan placed below the grill surface to catch fat, juices, and excessive basting sauces.

Grate. The metalwork holding the fuel in a smoker or barbecue.

Grill. The lattice of metal that the meat is placed upon for grilling or smoking. In a more general sense, the entire unit is called a grill or barbecue. As a verb, to cook over the direct heat of flames or coals.

Grill Brush. A brush with metal bristles used to clean the grill.

Instant-Read Thermometer. A probe temperature device that tells the internal temperature of grilled and smoked meats in seconds. Do not use as an oven thermometer.

Jerk. A style of smoke-grilling popular in Jamaica that uses an allspice and chile pepper–based marinade.

Marinade. A seasoned sauce that meat is soaked in prior to cooking to tenderize it.

Pig Pickin'. Hunks of meat that are sliced or pulled by hand from a pork shoulder.

Pit. A hole in the ground for cooking meats over coals or a manufactured unit for smoking meats.

Rub. A dry spice mixture rubbed over meat prior to cooking.

Skewer. A metal or bamboo stick used to grill kebabs, seafood, and vegetables.

Skirt Steak. Beef diaphragm muscle that is used for fajitas.

Slab of Ribs. The entire side of the rib cage.

Smoke Ring. The pink ring just below the surface of smoked meat that proves it is true barbecue.

Smoker. A metal unit for smoking meats by the indirect heat method.

Sop. A basting sauce applied to the meat during the cooking process. Also called mop.

Spareribs. The lower portion of a hog's ribs. This term refers only to pork ribs.

Resources

CHILES, HERBS, SPICES, HOT SAUCES, BARBECUE SAUCES,
AND OTHER INGREDIENTS

Frieda's, Inc.
4465 Corporate Center Drive
Los Alamitos, CA 90720
(800) 241-1771 or (714) 826-6100

Hot Sauce Harry's
3422 Flair Dr.
Dallas, TX 75229
(800) 588-8979 or (214) 902-8552

Melissa's Specialty Foods
P.O. Box 21127
Los Angeles, CA 90021
(800) 588-0151

Mo Hotta Mo Betta
P.O. Box 4136
San Luis Obispo, CA 93403
(800) 462-3220

Pendery's
1221 Manufacturing
Dallas, TX 75207
(800) 533-1870

Salsa Express
100 N. Tower Road
Alamo, TX 78516
(800) 43-SALSA

Santa Fe School of Cooking
116 W. San Francisco St.
Santa Fe, NM 87501
(505) 983-4511

continued on next page

CHILE SEED AND PLANT SOURCES

The Chile Woman
1704 South Weimer Rd.
Bloomington, IN 47403
(812) 332-8494

Cross Country Nurseries
P.O. Box 170
Rosemont, NJ 08556-0170
(908) 996-4646
www.chileplants.com

Enchanted Seeds
P.O. Box 6087
Las Cruces, NM 88006-6087
(505) 523-6085

GRILLS AND ACCESSORIES

Barbeques Galore
15041 Bake Pky., Suite A
Irvine, CA 92618
(800) 752-3085

Barbecue Pits by Klose
2214½ West 34th St.
Houston, TX 77018
(713) 686-8720
www.bbqpits.com

Chef's Catalogue
3215 Commercial Avenue
Northbrook, IL 60062-1900
(800) 338-3232

WEBSITES

The Barbecue Source (www.bbqsource.com). Offering spices, sauces, grills, and wood products, this is a comprehensive site. They also have a toll-free number, (888) 252-7686.

The Barbecue Store (www.barbecue-store.com). This retail site has a good selection of barbecue products and supplies. They also have a toll-free number, (888) 789-0650.

Barbecuen on the Web (www.barbecuen.com). Arguably the most complete barbecue site, Barbecuen has a retail store, tons of recipes, cook-off schedules, BBQ news, and lots more.

BBQ.COM (www.bbq.com). This site covers a wide range of barbecuing and grilling subjects, including grills, smokers, recipes, accessories, and even restaurant reviews.

Cookshack (www.cookshack.com). Both a manufacturer and retailer, Cookshack offers smokers, spices, woods, and accessories.

Fiery Foods & Barbecue Business Super Site (www.fiery-foods.com). This is mostly an industry site with business articles, but also has some consumer material.

Grilling Out (www.grillingout.com). A retailer of gas grills, including Weber, Viking, and Broilmaster, they also have a toll-free number, (877) MYGRILL.

Peppers.com (www.peppers.com). This site offers one of the largest collections of hot sauce for sale anywhere.

Bibliography

Adler, Karen. *Hooked on Fish on the Grill.* Kansas City: Pig Out Publications, 1992.

Auchmutey, Jim. "A Southern View on Barbecue." *Chile Pepper,* August 1996: 20.

Barnard, Melanie. *Low-Fat Grilling.* New York: HarperPerennial, 1995.

Beard, Henry and Roy McKie. *Cooking: A Cook's Dictionary.* New York: Workman, 1985.

Beard, James. *James Beard's Treasury of Outdoor Cooking.* New York: Golden Press, 1960.

———. *Barbecue with Beard.* New York: Golden Books, 1975.

Browne, Rick and Jack Bettridge. *Barbecue America.* Alexandria, VA: Time-Life Books, 1999.

Bush, T.L. *The Official Barbecue and Barbecue Sauce Cookbook.* Houston: Gulf Publishing, 1996.

Carpenter, Hugh and Teri Sandison. *The Great Ribs Book.* Berkeley, CA: Ten Speed Press, 1999.

Davis, Ardie A. *The Great BBQ Sauce Book.* Berkeley, CA: Ten Speed Press, 1999.

Davis, Rich and Shifra Stein. *Wild about Kansas City Barbecue.* Kansas City: Pig Out Publications, 1995.

DeWitt, Dave. *The Chile Pepper Encyclopedia.* New York: William Morrow & Co., 1999.

DeWitt, Dave and Paul W. Bosland. *The Pepper Garden.* Berkeley, CA: Ten Speed Press, 1993.

———. *Peppers of the World.* Berkeley, CA: Ten Speed Press, 1996.

DeWitt, Dave and Nancy Gerlach. *The Whole Chile Pepper Book.* Boston: Little, Brown, 1990.

———. *The Habanero Cookbook.* Berkeley, CA: Ten Speed Press, 1995.

DeWitt, Dave and Melissa T. Stock and Kellye Hunter. *The Healing Powers of Peppers.* New York: Three Rivers Press, 1998.

Dove, Laura. "BBQ—A Southern Cultural Icon." On World Wide Web at http://xroads.virginia.edu/~MA95/dove/bbq.html, no date but available in 1999.

Dozier, Susan. "In Hot Pursuit of BBQ Ribs." *Southern Living*, May 1990: 123.

Eckhardt, Linda West. *The Only Texas Cookbook*. New York: Grammercy Publishing, 1981.

Editors of Sunset Books. *Grill by the Book: Fish and Shellfish*. Menlo Park, CA: Sunset Publishing Corp., 1996.

——. *Grill by the Book: Steaks, Chops, and Burgers*. Menlo Park, CA: Sunset Publishing Corp., 1996.

Editors of *Sunset Magazine*. *Sunset Barbecue Cook Book*. Menlo Park, CA: Lane Publishing Company, 1959.

Elie, Lolis Eric. *Smokestack Lightening*. New York: Farrar, Straus and Giroux, 1996.

Famularo, Joe. *The Joy of Grilling*. Hauppauage, NY: Barron's Educational Series, 1988.

Fowler, Damon, ed. *Mrs. Hill's Southern Practical Cookery and Recipe Book*. Columbia: University of South Carolina Press, 1995.

Garner, Bob. *North Carolina Barbecue: Flavored by Time*. Winston-Salem, NC: John F. Blair, Publisher, 1997.

Geist, Willam. "Manly Chores." In *The Great Food Almanac*, by Irene Chalmers. San Francisco: Collins Publishers, 1994.

Greeley, Alexandra. *Asian Grills*. New York: Doubleday, 1993.

Hazen, Janet. *New Game Cuisine*. San Francisco: Chronicle Books, 1990.

Hearon, Reed. *La Parilla: The Mexican Grill*. San Francisco: Chronicle Books, 1996.

Hillman, Howard. *Kitchen Science*. Boston: Houghton Mifflin, 1981.

Jamison, Cheryl Alters and Bill Jamison. *Texas Home Cooking*. Boston: Harvard Common Press, 1993.

——. *Smoke & Spice*. Boston: Harvard Common Press, 1994.

——. *Born to Grill*. Boston: Harvard Common Press, 1998.

Johnson, Greg and Vince Staten. *Real Barbecue*. New York: Harper & Row, 1988.

Jones, Evan. *American Food*. Woodstock, NY: The Overlook Press, 1990.

Land, Mary. *Louisiana Cookery*. Baton Rouge: Louisiana State University Press, 1954.

Langer, Richard W. *Where There's Smoke, There's Flavor*. Boston: Little, Brown, 1996.

McCabe, Connie. "KC BBQ." *Saveur*, No. 27 (May/June 1998): 70.

McGee, Harold. *On Food and Cooking*. New York: Charles Scribner's Sons, 1984.

Neiman, Rachel. "BBQ Secrets of the Stars." *NoHo News* (North Hollywood, CA) Vol. 1, No. 1 (July, 1999): 4.

Permenter, Paris and John Bigley. *Texas Barbecue.* Kansas City: Pig Out
Publications, 1994.

Peyton, James W. *El Norte: The Cuisine of Northern Mexico.* Santa Fe, NM: Red
Crane Books, 1990.

———. *La Cocina de la Frontera: Mexican-American Cooking from the Southwest.*
Santa Fe, NM: Red Crane Books, 1994.

Raichlen, Steven. *The Barbecue Bible.* New York: Workman, 1998.

Robbins, Maria Polushkin. *A Cook's Alphabet of Quotations.* New York: Dutton
Books, 1991.

Root, Waverly and Richard de Rochemont. *Eating in America.* Hopewell, NJ: The
Ecco Press, 1995.

Rozin, Elisabeth. *The Primal Cheeseburger.* New York: Penguin Books, 1994.

———. *The Universal Kitchen.* New York: Penguin Books, 1996.

St. Laurent, Jonathan and Charles Neave. *Uncle Billy's Downeast Barbeque Book.*
West Rockport, ME: Dancing Bear Books, 1991.

Shahin, Jim. "Barbecue Capital of the World." *American Way,* May 15, 1996: 40.

Sinnes, A. Cort. *Gas Grill Gourmet.* Boston: Harvard Common Press, 1996.

Spears, Grady and Robb Walsh. *A Cowboy in the Kitchen.* Berkeley, CA: Ten Speed
Press, 1998.

Steingarten, Jeffrey. "Going Whole Hog." *Vogue,* September 1993: 536.

Stern, Jane and Michael. *Way Out West.* New York: HarperCollins, 1993.

Stock, Melissa T. and Kellye Hunter. "BBQ," *Chile Pepper,* July/August 1995: 24.

Sweet, Alexander and John Knox. *On a Mexican Mustang through Texas.* London,
1905 (out of print).

Tarantino, Jim. *Marinades.* Freedom, CA: The Crossing Press, 1992.

Taylor, Joe Grey. *Eating, Drinking and Visiting in the Old South.* Baton Rouge:
Louisiana State University Press, 1982.

Thorne, John. "Serious Pig." *Simple Cooking,* No. 23 (Summer/Autumn 1988): 1.

Tolbert, Francis X. *A Bowl of Red.* New York: Doubleday & Co., 1953.

Wason, Betty. *Cooks, Gluttons, and Gourmets.* Garden City, NY: Doubleday & Co.,
1962 (out of print).

Index